Dedicated to Olivia, Sofia and Tenley. Three of my most favourite people in the world. I hope that you will always know your value, and never settle for less than God's absolute best, because you're worth it. We all are.

Hannah and Nathan. I am so grateful you're in my life.

Kris, you were, and always will be, worth it all. Everything that lead to you, was completely worth it, and I'd do it all again, if it meant you at the end.

Table of Contents

i

ii

The Beautiful Art of Surrender

What would it be like, to hand everything important to me, over to God, trusting that He will take care of it *all?* To throw my hands in the air - like I just don't care - and say, *"Here, Lord, YOU deal with it!"* To completely surrender my will to His. To confidently rest and have perfect peace, despite all the unknowns.

Our brains are wired to avoid the unknown at all costs - because unknowns are *scary.* Still, not knowing what the future holds - or even our next step - yet, having faith strong enough to trust Him with every detail of our lives, not worrying about a thing... a worthy goal. I've been learning that despite having rough days/weeks/months, I don't have to be constantly reassured that He's taking care of me and my future. He's already proven over and over again that I can *always rely on Him.*

For a couple of years, I've been toying with the idea about writing about my personal healing process post-divorce. Understanding a possible tendency to throw my ex-husband under the bus (and the wisdom in not doing

1

so), I left the idea alone for a while. However, as the months passed, the call to write intensified.

"*Lord,*" I said, "*if you want me to write a book, what would You like it to be about? I've learned so much about myself, but there's so much of what I've gone through that I don't want to make public. As it is, I already regret sharing private information that I never should have!*"

His answer was clear: "Write about the process of surrendering."

Simple as that. Hmm, that is something I have definitely learned a lot about! First, I'll start with...

THE PROCESS OF COPING AND GETTING THROUGH

Growing up, I was a good Christian girl who rarely gave my parents grief, except for the occasional poor boyfriend choices during my teenage years. Who doesn't have a few of those experiences tucked in their back pocket?

My parents were - and still are - wonderful people who love the Lord with their whole heart. They were young when they had children (myself, one brother, and two sisters) and did their best to raise us in a loving, albeit conservative, environment. There was no alcohol or playing cards in our home, we weren't allowed to watch many TV shows like the Care Bears, Simpsons, Power Rangers, etc., or even attend school dances. They've loosened up over the years, realizing which battles were worth fighting and which weren't; alcohol still isn't allowed in their home, but we play cards all the time when we're there. I remember not being allowed to wear nail polish when I was small, but when my youngest sister was little, my dad would paint her fingernails. Being the oldest - and born twelve years apart - it was easy to see how much my parents changed during that time.

My parents are some of the most generous people I know; they would do anything for anyone. In the last few years, my dad has bailed me out more times than I can count. He has such a gentle, peaceful spirit, and it's hard to express how much I love and appreciate him. My mom's mother was a Pastor at a small Pentecostal church in the '70s, and that torch has now been passed on to her. Almost 60 years old now (my life may be on the line by revealing that!), my mom, who still claims she was a terrible student in school, is currently in the process of getting her Master's Degree in Christian Leadership. She doesn't realize it, but I hope one day she will know how much of a powerhouse she is, and the anointing God has placed on her. Looking back, I deeply appreciate the way I was raised - as well as the loving men and powerful women in my life.

I grew up loving Jesus, trying my best to "do right" as much as possible. Self-righteousness, judgement and I became pretty good friends in my late teens and early twenties. For example, if I was at someone's house and they were watching a movie that I deemed inappropriate, I'd leave - making sure they knew why! It's embarrassing when I think about it now, and I often wonder why people stayed friends with me back then.

I constantly stuck my foot in my mouth, seldom realizing it until months later. Once, while driving around with a couple of girls I didn't know that well, we discussed my getting a car before heading off to college later that summer. I mentioned that my dad had found an older Ford Taurus, and I complained about not wanting it because I considered it an "old grandma car." Guess what model of car I was sitting in... yep, you guessed it: an older Ford Taurus.

Seriously, if you asked anyone who knew me back then, they would likely tell you that I was a self-righteous know-it-all who constantly said stupid things. (If I could talk to any of them now, I'd apologize like no one's business, explaining that I'm not the same girl!) None of us are the same as we were 10-15 years ago - or even one year ago for that matter. Life has a way of changing and humbling us.

Jake[1] and I started dating in 2007, both at the ripe old age of 22. While many guys had shown an interest in me, Jake was the first one that seriously *interested me,* and for some reason, I was petrified that I'd grow old alone - so I jumped right in. We grew up on opposite sides of the country, but in much of the same conservative way. He knew all the old hymns and played guitar and bass at his church, which was something I was very excited about. *"You play on your worship team and know who the Gaither's are? Please, date me now!"*

I don't remember judging people for getting divorced, but I felt certain that it wouldn't ever be me. When Jake and I married (a year later), we both agreed that divorce wasn't a possibility. Ever.

Yet, eight-and-a-half years later - after a mostly unhappy marriage, and a month after I had given birth to our third

---

[1] Name has been changed.

daughter - that's exactly where I found myself. Alone, broken-hearted, completely lost; a place I never thought I'd be.

I won't be sharing many details of my marriage or divorce for a few reasons. First: those details don't matter. People get divorced for many different reasons, and I'd like my message to reach as many people as possible. The more specific my story, the less people I reach - and possibly, help. Even if you haven't been through a divorce, you've probably experienced another agonizing event in your life, and you may be struggling to surrender your heart - and unanswered questions - to the Lord. My message isn't about my divorce details; it's about how beautiful and hard the process of surrendering every single part of my life to Jesus has been, *and still is.*

Second, my ex-husband, Jake, and his family are private people, and I want to honour that. I love his family with all my heart - and always will.

Lastly - and most importantly - my daughters might read this one day; I want them to be able to learn about our story, still love and respect us both, and not be humiliated by any of our choices.

That said, I'll share that Jake made the decision to leave - and when he did, I was a wreck. I didn't eat for months and lost a ton of weight. My newborn, Tenley, was a bit pre-mature, and woke up every 45 minutes throughout the night *every night* for the first six months. I was running on no sleep. Once my morning alarm rang, I'd get Olivia (my oldest daughter, six, and in first grade), ready for school and then spend the rest of the day entertaining Sofia, my four-year-old middle daughter - all while taking care of a cranky newborn! Naps? I gave up on those, as it seemed that something always happened to prevent me from any helpful daytime respites. One afternoon, I decided to grab a little catnap, but the minute I closed my eyes, the house alarm (not turned on, or even plugged in) started beeping. *Of course!* I found it was easier to surrender to the idea of sleeplessness than to hope for it and be disappointed.

Olivia was an emotional wreck for a long time after our separation. Shortly after the split with Jake, she told one of my friends that she was so grief-stricken she didn't know if she could live anymore. Sofia was always hungry and emotional. Tenley was beyond fussy and never slept. I was falling apart from a broken heart. In the evenings, I would curl up in my rocking chair in the corner of my living room, and sob into a blanket. Even if Tenley did sleep, *I didn't,* because all I did was cry. Beyond any shadow of doubt, I know that God helped me, giving me enough energy to get through every day.

During the first five months at my new place, my dad finished up the basement so I could eventually find a renter. When my dad was working downstairs, he'd often hear a big commotion upstairs, and come up to find us all sobbing. He'd take Tenley, and walk around with her until she'd fall asleep in his arms. Then he'd make himself a cup of coffee and listen to me as I poured out the remnants of my angry, broken heart. I know how devastated he was about the whole situation, but he never showed it; he was always a great shoulder to cry on and my much-needed voice of reason. I lost count of the many, many times he was there for me. Not only was he available for me physically during the day, he also fixed my dishwasher three times, repaired two leaky toilets (twice), built gates for my fence, and helped me with other household issues. Once, I ran over something with my car, puncturing my gas tank and leaking gas everywhere. Dad picked the girls up, drove behind me all the way to the auto body shop, then took us all home. Another time, he came to the gas station to pay for my gas because I was on empty and had forgotten my wallet at home. Thank you, Dad, for the bond we shared during that time. It is sweet to see how close and protective he is to all of us now.

During the whole process of separation, my mom's retired cousin, Allan, became my best friend. He would come over for coffee and listen to me rant - often about the same things repeatedly. He never told me to get over it and move on; instead, his responses were always encouraging. He was such a gift to me during that time, and I'll forever be grateful.

Despite the help from Dad and Allan, I made things hard on myself by driving by or snooping in Jake's house, looking for clues as to what he was up to. I thought I needed to know. Then, I'd confront him with such anger that I couldn't think straight. In hindsight, I understand how often I let emotions control me, and I shouldn't have done half the things I did. Rifling through the house he lived in, the truck he drove, his phone bills and credit card statements... these were not effective or healthy ways to cope. While it's easy to see that now, in the heat of the moment, all I saw was *my pain.* I regret a lot of my actions, but they provided a vital learning experience; now I can share with others what NOT to do after a break-up! And while going through "his stuff" was legal (technically, it was still half-mine), going down that road was a mistake, and an invasion of his privacy and a painful, self-inflicted invasion of my peace.

In the year following our separation, I felt like God gave me dreams and words that our marriage would be reconciled. I clung to them like they were life. But when new information would come forward (like finding things in his house), the wound would open again, forcing a re-start of the whole grieving process. It was a vicious cycle that should have ended long before it did.

Six months after our initial separation, I was going through our old phone bills and discovered that there was another woman - and had been the entire time. The reason for our separation was finally brought to light. Again, I'm not sure why I thought I needed to go through old paperwork, and I don't know why I was so surprised and angry that he had moved on. But my heart was destroyed, again, and the reconciliation I was so sure God had promised me was even less possible.

That was the worst week of my life, but I felt entitled to treat myself - to eye lash extensions. I reacted terribly to the glue, my eyes swelled shut and felt like they were on fire. (A couple months later, a local radio station's Facebook page was hosting a contest for the most terrible picture, so I submitted a picture of myself after the eyelash debacle. I won by unanimous decision!) The day after my terrible reaction to the extensions, I realized that I needed to register Sofia for kindergarten; I wanted to get her in a specific kindergarten class, so I absolutely had to go *that day*. My eyes were still swollen almost shut, so I entered the school in sunglasses. I had all three girls with me, and Sofia decided to have a major screaming meltdown right in the middle of the office while I was trying to talk to the secretary (still in dark sunglasses). People were staring at us, me in sunglasses, Sofia rolling on the floor. I managed to keep it together until I got to the car - then I completely lost it.

The next day, my parents came over, witnessing *my* major meltdown. Mom assured me that I'd get through this, and when I did, I'd l look back at this week and laugh. While I didn't believe her then, I do look back and laugh now. I cry sometimes too. It was the absolute worst week of my life, and I thank God that He got me through it. (The school secretaries still remember me to this day - and I can't decide if that's a good thing or not.)

I wish I would have written down my thoughts and feelings more during that time, so I could look back, track progress, and see God at work. It's why I suggest that you write, *a lot.* Keep a journal and take notes every day. Sadly, all I did was cry; take care of my kids and cry. I didn't eat, didn't sleep, I just cried. Had I spent time journaling (instead of mentally mulling through thoughts,) I believe I'd have cried less.

At this point, I still felt like God still wanted me to pray for reconciliation; it was confusing, and still confuses me now. I'd have dreams, and I felt Him tell me that I still needed to honour Jake because he was still - technically - my husband. Sometimes scripture would speak to me about God restoring and healing people and relationships. I'd teeter-totter between being angry and hopeful. Back and forth. Back and forth.

The Sunday before I found out he was dating someone, I went up to the front of my very small church for prayer, telling the Lord I wanted to know Him better. Then, *the day after I found out,* I felt the Lord tell me that Jake was going to go through some hard times, and I was supposed to be there for him. My first response was to laugh, secretly hoping he suffered! After some prayer, I told the Lord, *"I hope You realize what You're asking me to do."*

His reply: "It's nothing I wouldn't do for you."

"Yes, but…"

"But nothing. You wanted to get to know Me better, well that's Me. I'm there for the people who don't deserve it. I'm kind to the unkind, I honour the un-honourable, I'm self-less to the selfish, I love the unlovable. And you being these things to him, is really getting to know My character."

Well, alright, then.

Accepting the death of my marriage was something I struggled to do, and for months I was painfully confused about why God would give me these promises - and then not follow through. Scripture says **His word never returns void** (Isa. 55:11 (NKJV)), and all His promises are yes and amen (2 Cor 1:20 (NKJV)). So, did I misunderstand His words to me? So many times? Was I the one who ruined the promises by not speaking life, but instead speaking death out of anger? Even now, almost three years later, I sometimes wonder why I felt so strongly that God wanted me to pray for my marriage. I've come to believe that God asked me to pray for the restoration of our marriage so I would learn to fully

15

depend on Him for help and comfort, instead of depending on - or rebounding to - another relationship with someone else. THAT would have been much, much easier to do, and I'd have likely done it many times.

Countless evenings during the last part of 2016 and almost the entire year of 2017, I found myself curled up in a corner, sobbing, asking God, *"Why me?"* It's natural for us to want to play the victim card. *"What did I do to deserve this? Why is this happening? God, why do You hate me?"* It's embarrassing to admit that I asked Him that many times, as if I was the only one in the world going through such heartache.

At one point during 2017, I was at an all-time low. I was in such a terrible emotional state that - for whatever reason - I thought it would be appropriate to vent to my little sister's friend, who was young and had never dated anyone before. Oddly, she asked me the most profound question, changing everything for me.

She said, "What did he contribute to your marriage that you're going to miss?" I sat there for a while, trying to think of something, but couldn't. At that point, I realized

16

that we had never been right for each other. Aside from our children, we had nothing in common. We lived completely different lives and neither of us were happy. Don't get me wrong, those aren't reasons to leave a marriage, but they were reason enough for me to try to let it go. Besides, at that point, I didn't have another option.

From that day forward, I began to evolve from an angry, entitled mentality to one who asked God, *"Ok, what are You trying teach me? What can I learn? You make all things work together for good, so how are You going to do that here?"*

Conversations with Sofia

Age: 5.5

> *Olivia and Sofia are sleeping with me in my bed. As I'm lying beside them, I hear:*
>
> *Olivia - Sofia, I have no room, move over!*
>
> *Sofia - I would, but mom has a big body, so...*

THE PROCESS OF SURRENDERING EVERYTHING

SURRENDERING THE HEALING PROCESS

Surrendering My Broken Heart / Knowing If - and When - to Move On

In January 2018, I asked the Lord to give me a theme word for the year. "Surrender" was His reply. What does it mean to surrender?

In a nutshell, it means to completely give up my will (what I *want* to do), and align my beliefs, thoughts, actions, *everything* to God and His will. I realized that the year would be full of things I'd have to learn how to surrender. It wasn't easy, and every day I surrendered my broken heart, my disappointments, my questions, my hurts, and my regrets. The promises, the doubt, the faith, the anger, the confusion. I surrendered my dream of having a perfect happy loving family. So many times, each day, I laid it all at the feet of Jesus, asking Him to take it all.

Starting first thing every morning, *"Ok Lord, I surrender it all to You."* And I'd name certain things I knew I needed to release at that particular time. I wasn't even out of bed before I unintentionally took most of it back, spending time worrying and crying over it.

Oh, right, *surrender.*

"Ok Lord, I'm giving it to You to take care of, again."

By lunch time I gave it all to God, taking it all back about a half-dozen times. Then a few more times by supper, depending on how distracted I was with the day's activities. Then a few more times in the evening, and even into the night. Questioning, worrying, regretting, wondering what I could have done - or could do now - to make it better. Every time I came face to face with all these questions, the Holy Spirit would gently remind me that I can't change the past, so the only thing to do now is surrender.

When we do fully surrender, we can rest in knowing He's there to take all our past hurts, mistakes, and everything else, exchanging them for peace, joy, love, and new life. Ninety-nine percent of the time, life doesn't turn out the way we thought it would - or should. Still, God is always, *always* good and always, *always* has our back.

I didn't know at what point I should stop praying for my marriage and move on. I knew God doesn't like divorce, and I knew He is capable of healing and restoring something or someone. I had seen people pray for their marriages, and sometimes He would bring couples back together. If I stopped praying for my marriage, did that mean I no longer believed God was able to heal it? Did it mean I had lost faith in His abilities? *I needed to surrender all these questions, too.*

I don't know why He heals some people and not others, and I don't know why He brings some couples back together and not others. If He gives us all free will, why do we pray for Him to change people's hearts?

Oh, all the questions! One thing I do know: God will always love us, He always has our best interests at heart,

He is always good, always faithful, and if we surrender everything to Him and trust Him, He will work it all out for the best. We must stay open to whatever that might look like; more than likely, it's going to look different than what we pictured!

The perfect family, the nice house with the white picket fence in a good neighbourhood that you always thought you wanted... that may not be what God had in mind for you. Maybe He made you to be more of a loft-in-the-city kind of person, with two dogs and a goldfish. Perhaps something terrible happened in your childhood that wasn't God's perfect plan for you, but He wants you to surrender it so He can use your story to help other people be healed and set free. Maybe your dream of an amazing modelling or sports career abruptly ended because of a freak accident, and now you must choose between being angry and bitter about it - or using your platform to show the world what *inward beauty* looks like. Or perhaps someone you love passed away, and you feel like you just can't go on anymore. Possibly, you're in a loveless marriage and you don't know what to do or how to pray. Maybe you, too, are struggling with being a newly single mom, and can't see the light at the end of the tunnel or find His grace anywhere in your mess. But I promise, there is an end to the darkness.

My prayer became: *"God, I know You're good. I know Your plans for me are good. Whatever they are, I'm open and willing to them. I completely surrender everything to You, and I trust You, no matter what the outcome is."*

Not long after I started praying that, I felt emotionally ready to move on. I decided to wait on dating others until I was legally divorced, believing it to be the right thing to do. By the end of 2018 (ten months after we filed for divorce, and over two years after our initial separation), our divorce became final; I knew I was free to move on in every way. When I received the divorce papers in the mail, I cried out of sadness because it was over. I also let out a huge sigh of relief because it was over.

Surrendering My Un-forgiveness

The struggle with un-forgiveness is hard. It can destroy our emotional and mental clarity, do damage to our physical bodies, and more importantly, it can (and does) hinder our relationship with God. It is vital to our spiritual lives that we forgive anyone who's wronged us, no matter what they've done. The reason is simple: Jesus forgives us of everything we've done, so we must forgive others of everything they've done. He also loves us unconditionally, forgives over and over, and keeps no record of wrongs. We are called to do likewise.

Wow - not going to lie - those things are all so hard to do! *Thank You, Lord, for Your grace to help us!*

Without going into details of my marriage, I'll say that I had to forgive... a few times. I remember many nights asking God if I should leave; He always replied with "Love always forgives and keeps no record of wrong." *Great. Awesome. That's exactly what I want to do right now.* Looking back, I'm glad we worked things out each time, because I would not be where I am today if I had left the marriage at any point. I wouldn't have all the kids I have, and I wouldn't have the house or car I have. I see how God's timing worked in it all, no matter how heartbreaking it was.

I also remember exactly where I was when God asked me to forgive Jake completely. It was in the spring of 2017, seven months after he had left me. The month prior, I had found out about his girlfriend, and was still emotional about that. I fasted for ten days - not certain why - and at the end of the fast, I realized why: I needed to forgive. I tried, but it was a very long and painful process.

I had to surrender my un-forgiveness to God many, many times. We cannot completely forgive in our own strength, we must allow God to help us, remaining open to how He'd like us to do it. For me, anger and bitterness came often, and I'd have to pray, hand it to God, and let HIM deal with it.

Regrettably, I often did that (handed it to God), *after* I had talked to other people and overshared things I had no business sharing, like how terrible Jake was, things he had done or said, and how angry I was. It took another year-and-a-half to learn that a big part of forgiveness entails *not keeping any records of wrongs.* That included sharing those wrongs with others.

One night, I heard God say, "If you've forgiven him, like you said you have, then it's done, it's over. When someone asks Me for forgiveness, I don't tell others about it, but I completely forgive and then forget it ever happened. And whether he's asked for your forgiveness, you've still forgiven him. Anything done in the past has to stay there. You can't continue to remind others about it or continue playing the victim card. That goes for anyone else that may have wronged you, as well."

"God, I'm really going to need Your grace to help me with that. That's something I definitely can't do on my own. You know I'm really struggling with telling others everything and playing the victim."

"I know. I'll help you and give you wisdom when you need it."

Since that time, I've been learning to surrender my words to the Lord, asking for wisdom whenever I'm in a situation - or know I'm going to be in a situation - where I could overshare. It's been hard, and I've failed many times, but I'm slowly learning to listen to those checks in my spirit, telling me to be quiet, and keep the past in the past.

Forgiveness is a matter of the heart, and when we forgive completely, our hearts are free. We can live in complete joy and peace because the past doesn't matter. We're not angry, we don't seek vengeance. When Jesus told us to forgive others, it was entirely for our benefit. He wants us to live in the fullness of freedom, love, peace and joy that He died to give us.

Disclaimer - If you are in an abusive, destructive, or toxic marriage, forgiving and keeping no record of wrongs does NOT MEAN you should stay with them. You can forgive that person, but love and respect yourself enough remove yourself (and children) from that toxic environment. Every situation is different and must be covered in prayer - lots

and lots of prayer. The safety and well-being of yourself
and your children is very important.

Scripture isn't always crystal clear about divorce and remarriage, especially in light of any kind of abuse. Theologically, it's a touchy subject, and people in the Church have been debating about it for centuries and, sadly, scripture has been used as a tool to manipulate women to stay in dangerous marriages. Jesus loved all women during His time on earth, clearly showing women how to be lovingly cherished and respected, displaying this countless times throughout the Gospels. He wants us to flourish, and no woman has ever flourished while under oppression: physically, emotionally, or spiritually. The theological take on divorce and remarriage may be confusing; maybe it's not as black and white as we think. Maybe it is a grey area.

Forgiveness, though, is <u>very</u> black and white.

Conversations with Sofia

Age: 5

> *Me - (On the way home from school) Sofia, how was school today?*
>
> *Sofia - I have no idea!*

Surrendering My Time in the Wilderness

In the last couple of years, I've spent many days desperately trying to get out of my wilderness. "Wilderness" is a period in which we experience a very dry, low, or hard time - either spiritually, emotionally, or physically. We must go through these times because they are seasons of preparation or growth; we need to experience them to move forward and be closer in our walk with the Lord. These places are where we develop and strengthen our roots, so to speak. I've often asked God what I could do to get out of there more quickly! To which He always replies: "Rest, wait, worship, trust Me, have peace, be still..."

Ugh, not that again.

I recently read a fantastic book (by John Bevere) about being in the wilderness: *God, Where are You?!*[2] Having spent so much time in my wilderness (and trying to pray

---

[2] Bevere, John. *God, Where are You?!* Palmer Lake, CO: Messenger International, Inc., 2019. www.MessengerInternational.org

my way out of it), this book was like water to my soul, confirming many things I felt the Lord was telling me. For example, God had given me some promises; this wilderness was part of the preparation for these promises. The loudest lesson to me was when you're in a wilderness, don't look for a way out. Instead, look for the Father's heart, getting as close to Him as you can, embracing your time there, because it is *always a necessary time.*

Going through my own wilderness, I remember King David from the Old Testament. As a teenager, he was anointed to be the next King of Israel, but was forced to run away, spending years and years not only in a physical wilderness, but also in an emotional wilderness. As time went on, his spiritual relationship with the Father deepened. He was known as "a man after God's heart" because in his difficult seasons, he learned to trust his Heavenly Father completely, surrendering everything to Him. Every battle started in prayer, with David inquiring of the Lord. Every time his heart was broken, he surrendered it to God. He was the greatest King of Israel because of what he learned from his time in the wilderness. We, too, must go through the wilderness, learn as much as we can, getting as close to the Lord as we can. As life has it, we'll all be going through more than one wilderness; might as well make the best of them!

Shortly after Jake's departure, it felt like God told me that I was headed down into a deep canyon, and it would be a long, very painful process. "But," He said, "there's water down there." I saw a picture of myself deep in the bottom of a dry canyon, recouping on a lawn chair by a stream. I didn't know what the water meant, but just two days later, I was listening to a message by Bill Johnson, who said that when the Bible speaks of water, usually it's referring to the Holy Spirit. I knew that was for me. I knew that even though the Holy Spirit was already comforting me, He would be more than just my comforter upon arrival at the bottom of that canyon. He'd be my *only source of survival.*

A few months later, when I found out about Jake's girlfriend, I reached that bottom. I was at the lowest point I had ever been in my life, and when I asked the

Lord if I was at the bottom, His voice was clear: "You're there, and you can stay and rest a while."

Two years later, I dreamed I was in a wilderness, pacing frantically and looking for a way out. I felt I needed to calm down - and I would, for a short time. Then, it was back to, "I've got to get out of here!" More frantic searching and pacing. As I was standing in my wilderness, unsure of what to do or where to go, I heard a voice telling me that there was nothing I could do to get out of it; only God could bring me out. And He would, when I was ready.

When I awoke, I called out in prayer: *"Ok God, I surrender this time in my wilderness to You. You've been so good to me so far and I trust that You're taking care of me, so I'll try my best to be patient while I'm here. Please help me when I can't do it on my own."*

We live in such an instant-gratification world; we want the challenging seasons of life to go by quickly. Five thousand years ago, pregnancy lasted nine months. No matter how many strides we've made in technology, pregnancy still lasts nine months. Premature babies can survive with less than a nine month gestation, much more often than they could 100 years ago, but it's still best if they can make it full-term. It works the same way with God. As people are called into higher levels of ministry - or even success - there is always a season or two of preparation beforehand. If a person tries to bypass that preparation, process, or wilderness, they will find they aren't equipped to handle that promise, ministry, or promotion as well.

If you are experiencing a wilderness and don't know how to cope, take this time to get to know the heart of the Father. Get to know yourself. Spend as much time as you possibly can in thanksgiving, worship and prayer. Read the Bible as if you were starving and it was the most delicious meal you've ever tasted. Find out who God wants to be for you, and you'll experience His goodness like you never have before. You'll learn that His intentions and nature toward you is better than you ever thought possible.

About six months ago, the Lord said to me, "A lot of people are going through a season of preparation, because when I unveil my power, I need to know who will be able to handle it." I think about the book of Acts in the New Testament; God poured His Spirit out on many people, signs and wonders were performed everywhere, and thousands were added to the church daily. But in all of that, there was still massive persecution and hard times. We need to learn to do signs and wonders in these last days (without arrogance and haughtiness), and should persecution come, we also need to be strong enough to stand in love and unity. After all, isn't that why we are here in the first place? To be Jesus to the world and to share His heart? But how can we, if we don't know ourselves, what His heart looks like?

Surrendering My Speech and Desire for Wisdom

I felt so devastated, betrayed, and humiliated during my separation, that a great deal of my grieving process was spent externally processing to everyone. I felt as if I owed people an explanation as to what happened and why. While I hated that I talked so openly about it, I just couldn't stop - no matter how hard I tried. I'd been an "oversharer" since I was a little girl, and it was something I was known for.

Every time I made things hard for myself (i.e., going through his house or bank statements), I shared what I discovered with anyone I thought would listen and care. In Jake's words, I was just embarrassing myself. Of course, I didn't see it that way until months later when the emotional dust had settled.

During 2017, I was part of a girls group that met once a month just to hang out and have adult time. Through my own fault, a lot of our conversation was about what I was going through; I couldn't see past the nose on my own face to ask how any of the other girls were doing. They chimed in here and there about their life, but there should have been more time geared to the rest of them, instead of me. Granted, no one else was going through what I was, but still... *Candice, can you just stop talking about yourself for even just a minute?*

I deeply regret sharing so much with people for a few reasons. First, it negatively affected a lot more people than I realized, and I didn't understand that until someone finally confronted me. Most conversations we have, come full circle, whether we want them to or not. In my grief and anger, I was saying awful things about people I loved, things I regret, and words I should have never uttered. Sometimes, once relationships are damaged, it takes a long time to repair and build that trust again - if it's even possible. Sadly, in most cases, the relationship is *never the same.*

Secondly, once people knew about what was happening in my life, they treated me differently, even avoiding me. Of the people who knew, very few deeply cared for me, staying by my side until the end. Many people *tried* to care, but quickly became bored or too busy. Some pretended to care because they wanted to hear a juicy story, but then proceeded to tell others about it. (I'm in no place to judge anyone for any of these behaviours, as I've done all of them at different points in my life.)

One day, I hope to say that I don't struggle with over-sharing, but instead, always use wisdom when I speak. While I'm a lot better now than I was (even a year ago), I am a slow work in progress. I suspect that is why God has separated me from most people, why I've had so much alone-time, so that I'll learn to talk *to Him about everything first*, instead of everyone else. It's one thing to talk a lot - many of us do - but it's another thing to over-share private information that is no one else's business but yours and the people directly involved.

Aside from those closest to you, no one else deserves - or needs - explanations about your situation or your life. I have learned the hard way: God wants us to talk to Him first. About everything. He genuinely cares about every detail of our lives! I've found that if I talk to Him about things first, He imparts wisdom and peace about the situation; something that no conversation with others could ever provide. I'm also learning that if I've truly forgiven someone, there's no need to broadcast their mistakes to others.

That said, God puts people in our lives with whom we can talk and learn from. Look for one or two solid people you know you can trust to be there, give you wise, unbiased advice, and who won't share your secrets with others. Tell them everything; tell everyone else the bare minimum. Above all (and for the love of all that is good), keep the details of your private life off social media! (Fortunately, I followed this advice, and am beyond glad that I did.)

The Lord has been speaking to me lately about guarding my words. Proverbs 18:21 (NKJV) says that "death and life are in the power of the tongue." James 3:8 says that the tongue can never be tamed, with the rest of the book going on to say how it important it is to guard what you say. We can't bless God and curse people with the same mouth.

He's also been speaking to me in dreams recently - which has been a lot of fun. There were so many things I didn't understand, so I bought an in-depth dream dictionary, which I can't get enough of! A couple weeks ago I had a dream that I was taken up in space and was fully wrapped in God's beautiful, peaceful presence. Afterward, I was breathing out fire and burning up wooden chairs. As I started breathing out these little flames, I thought to myself that I'd get better with practice, and I believe these flames meant I was speaking God's Word over people. Immediately after I had that thought about practicing, while still sleeping, I felt the Holy Spirit impress on me that I MUST be very careful with my words because of the weight they carry. That's the case for ALL of us. Our spoken words have weight, they mean something, what we say *matters.* Aside from the scriptures I shared above, here's why:

Angels and demons constantly hear every word we say. If we start speaking the Word of God and our vocabulary is in agreement with the Word of God, it activates the power of God and empowers the angels to encamp around us and to prepare the way for the destiny that God has for us. When we start speaking death, curses, or doubt, it empowers demons to respond and gives them the right to bring havoc into our lives, to strike us and steer us off God's path. Our victory is in being in harmony with God's Word.[3]

This paragraph speaks to me so much! I never want to give the enemy the right to hurt people or myself, based on what I say.

"Lord, I surrender my words to You. Please show me Your heart toward myself and others. Give me wisdom and love to believe it and share it."

---

[3] Thompson, Adam F. and Adrian Beale. *The Divinity Code To Understanding your Dreams and Visions.* Shippensburg, PA: Destiny Image Publishers, Inc., 2011

Conversations with Sofia

Age: 5

> *Olivia and Sofia were arguing about something this evening...*
>
> *Sofia to Olivia - I DON'T CARE ABOUT ANYFING EXCEPT GOD AND MY WEGO!*

Surrendering My Springtime

There's a light at the end of every tunnel, a silver lining to every cloud, a springtime to every winter. Sometimes, the darkness lasts for longer than we'd like, but that just makes us more thankful for the light.

In October 2018, God told me my theme word for 2019 would be "New Beginnings." I knew that things were going to finally change for the better; I was very excited. I started counting down the days until the New Year. *67 days to go! Woohoo!* January came and went, and nothing really happened.

Umm, ok, maybe February is my month?

I decided to book a quick trip for the first weekend in February, to Redding, California. I wanted to visit a friend and finally check out where my favourite music and podcasts come from: Bethel Church.[4] It was so encouraging to see what God was doing there and how

---

[4] For all things Bethel Church, visit www.Bethel.com.

people's lives were being changed. During the Friday night service, two different people prayed over me, at different times, and both told me that they felt like God wanted me to know that it's springtime! EXCITING! Spring signifies new life and new beginnings, and I couldn't wait for it all to happen.

As I write this, it's the third week of March, 2019. In northern Alberta, the weather this time of year could be anywhere from minus 30 degrees Celsius (with copious amounts of snow) to what we consider tropical weather: anything above freezing. Yesterday it was plus twelve degrees; which is shorts and T-shirt weather with puddles from melted snow everywhere. It was so gorgeous out that I went to my girls' parent-teacher interviews in a T-shirt. I didn't even take a sweater, and I take a sweater *everywhere*.

My favourite part of spring - aside from the warmer weather - is that our days get longer and longer. In the winter, the sun comes up around 9:00 am and starts going down by 4:00 pm. In the summer, the sun is up by 4:00 am and doesn't start going down until 11:00 pm.

It's wonderful! On the summer solstice, the sun is only down (completely dark outside) for maybe an hour.

There are so many aspects of springtime that I've never really thought about or paid attention to - until this year. Here, the first couple months of spring are messy. The mountains of snow are melting and leaving puddles everywhere. It's filthy from all the salt and sand sprayed on the icy roads during the winter, so there's sand, dirt, and rocks far and wide. No vehicle can stay clean for more than 30 seconds, and your windshield doesn't stand a chance against all the rock chips from the dirty semi-trucks on the highway, returning from working in the "bush." (The bush is considered anything off the highway that truckers must drive in and out of. Because we live on oil and natural gas reserves - and the wells are in the middle of the bush - truckers must drive to and from these sites every day. Many of the roads are all ice in the winter - which melts in the spring. This time of the year is called "spring break up," and these roads can't be driven on by large trucks during certain times of the day - or at all - until they completely melt. All in all, it's very messy!)

Front lawns are covered in dirty snow mountains, piled high from all the road clearing done during winter. Once it melts, lawns need to be cleaned, raked, and fertilized to get some life back into them. Old snow (from the earliest snow falls) is the last to melt, so it becomes moldy before it melts, bringing out terrible allergies in people. Wait, it gets better. Once the snow is finally gone, you can see - everywhere - just *how messy people are* by all the garbage left behind that the snow once covered. People are swerving all over the roads to avoid the potholes left everywhere from the extreme temperature changes. Like little mini canyons everywhere. It really is a magical time.

There's absolutely no point to plant any flowers before May long weekend (the third weekend in May) because the weather is so unpredictable; anything planted before then will likely freeze during the night. A few years ago, I bought some beautiful pink and purple flowered hanging baskets, bringing them in every night so they wouldn't freeze. I forgot about them one night, and that was the end of that! Last year I started "planting" fake flowers from Ikea, outside, which are beautiful all year long, maintenance free, and never die! Genius?! Yes, I know!

I really do love spring, despite its messiness here. Days are getting warmer, people are coming out of hibernation and spending time outside, and the sound of kids playing together, riding their bikes, jumping in puddles - it's so much fun! Sofia and all the other neighbourhood kids go from house to house, or backyard to backyard, playing and having a field day from morning until bedtime. Many of the parents bought their kids walkie-talkies so they could see where they were or tell them it was time to come home.

All of this has been making me wonder about how this "springtime" in my own life is going to be. Will it be as messy as our Northern Alberta spring? Once the "snow" melts, is it going to reveal a bunch of dirt and garbage that was hidden underneath? Is it going to be beautiful and warm during the "day" but still cold during the darkness? Like all the new life that comes with spring, what new life or new beginnings will come for me? Will it be as beautiful and wonderful as the flowers that bloom and the trees that blossom?

I'm excited for this new season in my life, though I have no idea what it will look like. I know it will be amazing, whatever it is. I feel like I'm right on the cusp of something big; God is about to move in a huge way and I'm holding my breath, waiting for it to happen. I can feel it deep down in my soul that He's about to move and do something amazing. I'm like a little kid, waiting for Christmas morning.

I'm trying to surrender my anticipation to God. I want to know what's going to happen -and when - so I can make a plan. God has been killing my flesh with all these unknowns, and the administrator in me is having a heart attack, while the other parts of me are trying to wait patiently for the Lord, trying to rest in His peace.

"So. Lord, if You could just do what only You can do, as soon as possible, that'd be great. In Your perfect timing, of course. But tomorrow would be awesome. Also, could You fill me in on Your plans? Even a general idea would be good. With a few detailed notes for each subject.

Nothing fancy, point form would even be fine. Just make sure to include dates and times of each event, and people involved. Or, I suppose You could do it Your way, where You just do it and don't tell me anything about it. Sure, I guess that works just as well... I'll just be waiting over here, ever so patiently."

All kidding aside, sometimes my prayers sound like that. What I really mean to say is this: *"God, I'm getting to know Your nature, and I know You are faithful, good, and kind. You love and value me more than I will ever comprehend. I know the purposes of your wildernesses are to reveal Your heart and prepare me for greatness. Everything You do has a purpose and You make all things work together for good. So, Jesus, I will trust that whatever is next for me is wonderful and perfect. Whatever my "spring" looks like, I know it will be exactly what I need at exactly the right time. I completely surrender my will to Yours. And when I feel overwhelmed and impatient, please give me grace to get through."*

I pray this often - more than once or twice per day. Surrendering is not a one-time event. Just like when we decide to change our diet and must be deliberate about how we eat all day, every day, we must also be intentional, making the decision to surrender everything at all times, day or night.

Conversations with Sofia

Age: 4.5

We're hanging out colouring and listening to Pentatonix when Sofia says:

I love Pentatonix. My favourite is the girl, because the boys water my eyes.

SURRENDERING MY FEELINGS AND EMOTIONS

Surrendering My Feelings of Inadequacy and Not Being Good Enough

I have absolutely no business writing a book. I'm not known for anything and I'm not part of a popular group. I tend to start - not finish - things, which is one of the reasons why I haven't told anyone I'm in the process of writing this book. I'm a bit afraid that people might laugh, thinking it's a dumb idea. Who would even read it? Who cares? Also, there's only a million other books about healing, going through different processes, surrendering... mine wouldn't possibly make a difference to anyone, would it?

When I was in university, I asked my brilliant roommate to edit one of my papers; she laughed at me for how poorly written it was. So the thought of handing this to an editor is terrifying.

Should I be trying to find a "real" job instead of writing?

But something happens when you surrender your entire will to Jesus and step out in obedience. None of those things matter. If He tells me to publish, I will. Whether it sells one copy or one million copies, it doesn't matter... that much. The important thing is that I am obedient. I will write what I can, then surrender the rest of it to the Lord to do with it what He wants.

Sometimes I forget and get discouraged about what I believe God wants me to do. OK, I *often* forget, especially when I open my computer to write. When I'm cleaning my house or doing something with my family, I feel like I should be writing. When I'm writing, I feel that I should be cleaning my house or spending time with my family. The teeter-totter - again. What do we do with that? Self-encourage! I am not crazy for doing what God has called me to do, and just when I think I'm in over my head (and can no longer be the one to encourage myself), God always finds a way to reassure me.

A few months ago, my mom's cousin, Carol, came to visit and had a word from the Lord for me. It was great timing because I was struggling with feelings of guilt and inadequacy, having prayed for 2 straight days seeking God's direction. I remember crying quietly, *"God, I need you to help me. I really need some encouragement. Please, just give me something!"* A few minutes later, while still praying, my mom texted to say that Carol had left a note for me at her house a few nights before. I asked her to send me a picture of it. It said:

Don't think God has abandoned you or that He doesn't care about you at this time. The Holy Spirit brought me to Proverbs 31, saying "Tell her to read it out loud and use her name in exchange for the word 'she'." What an amazing woman Proverbs 31 describes, what an amazing woman you are, even raising up more amazing women. You are mine.

Wow. God is so good, so faithful. The first time I read the Proverbs passage out loud, I had a tough time using my name; I didn't feel like I represented that woman, or that I deserved to be held in such high esteem. But God is helping me see that I AM becoming stronger, wiser, and kinder as the days go on. In The Passion

Translation, verse Proverbs 31:10 reads: "She is a woman of strength and mighty valor!" In the footnote, the translator states that the word used to describe this woman also means "mighty; wealthy; excellent; morally righteous; full of substance, integrity, abilities, and strength; mighty like an army."[5]

That verse didn't register fully with me until recently, when I returned to the words spoken over me while I was in Redding. My friend had taken me to another friend's house to watch the Superbowl; the owners were a wonderful couple who took a keen interest in the lives of younger people. He asked me what I wanted to do with my future. I don't think he realized I was in my mid-thirties; his draw dropped when I said *"Well, I'm a single mom of three little girls - so I'm just trying to navigate my present."*

Before the conversation ended, he said, "I want to pray for you before you leave for the airport, would that be

---

[5] Simmons, Dr. Brian. *The Passion Translation.* BroadStreet Publishing Group, LLC, 2017, pg 283.

okay?" Of course, I agreed... I'll take all the prayer I can get!

Just before I headed out, they paused the game, and everyone gathered around me to pray. As this was happening, a young girl said that she felt the Lord urging her to tell me that I am more than my stature, I'm stronger and more powerful than I think I am, the weight and glory I carry is mighty, and there is so much authority walking behind me, in everything. I knew God was all over those words! She had no idea of the story behind them, how I fight feelings of being small and insignificant daily, and how I often feel like a child who can't do much. Despite everything I've gone through, in a room full of women my age, I still feel like the little kid that doesn't belong.

I'm working diligently to put the verse in Proverbs and this prophetic word together, making it a platform on which I can firmly stand. I'm surrendering my thoughts about myself, to God, and trying to see myself the way He sees me. I can know my identity and who I am, how strong I am, and with Him, be capable of more than I ever thought possible. And the greatest part of that? *You are, too!* You are stronger than you think you are. You are amazing and capable of so many wonderful things. You are loved incredibly so much by the Father, that He paid the ultimate price of His son, just for you!

*Side note: My favourite part of this whole writing process happened when I was about three quarters of the way through writing. My church was hosting a special service with a speaker from Washington State. Neither him nor I knew each other, but as soon as I sat down beside him, he looked at me and said, "God wants you to write a book! The Bride of Christ needs to read it!" I was so taken aback and happy that I almost started bawling right then and there. I already knew in my heart that I was doing what God wanted me to do, by writing this book. But God knew all of the insecurities I was struggling with, and knew I needed such a huge confirmation from someone on the "outside".

Surrendering My Loneliness

My favourite movie is "The Holiday," and I've watched it more times than I can count. Both Kate Winslet's character (Iris) and Cameron Diaz's character (Amanda) describe my life perfectly, except for the ending, since I'm not there yet. I especially identify with a conversation between Iris and Miles (Jack Black) after Miles has discovered that his girlfriend is cheating on him. In response to his question about why he always falls for the bad girl, Iris says, "Because you're hoping you're wrong, and every time she does something that tells you she's no good, you ignore it. And every time she comes through and surprises you, she wins you over, and you lose that argument with yourself, that she's not for you."[6] Wiser words were never spoken, and it's likely that nearly everyone in the world has done this with at least one relationship! Sadly, some of us need to go through

---

[6] *The Holiday.* Written and Directed by Nancy Meyers. Columbia Pictures. 2006. 1:36:50

a couple of poor relationships, so we don't take advantage of a good one *when it does come along.*

Iris goes on to tell him about the guy she's trying to get over and how she understands the feeling of being small and so insignificant that you ache in places you didn't know were there. And it doesn't matter what you do to try to get over it, she explains, "You still go to bed every night going over every detail, wondering what you did wrong or how you could have misunderstood. Or how you could have thought you were that happy or try and convince yourself he'll see the light and show up at your door..."[7] Not unlike this movie, my life - and maybe yours - seems to be a story of unrequited love. Still, this quote speaks to me because she puts words to the pain I've felt - but have been unable to express. Plus, she normalizes it, because so many other people have gone through the same thing and have felt the same way. It's

---

[7] *The Holiday.* Written and Directed by Nancy Meyers. Columbia Pictures. 2006. 1:38:45

not only *okay* to go through this process, but it's also *normal*. Thank goodness!

I feel like loneliness from divorce is different from other types. I'm not undermining the other kinds of loneliness; I'm just saying it's different and can be both more and less stressful *if you do it right*. I see countless couples get divorced, moving on to someone else so quickly that they forego taking time for themselves to heal, to figure out their life, issues - and everything else. I'll say it: moving on to another person right away is a cop-out, and not healthy for anyone. No person can mend another's broken heart; no relationship will do that for you. If you are divorced - or go through a breakup - you must take time to heal properly. Spend quality time figuring out who you are, what you want out of life, what your goals are, and what changes you need to make in yourself to be better. Most importantly, you must figure out how to love yourself and see yourself as an amazing person whom God unconditionally loves and adores.

Determining exactly WHO God is to you (and for you) is also equivalent in learning to love yourself. For me, He is everything. Psalm 23 (TPT, paraphrased), says that the Lord is my shepherd and my best friend. Being my shepherd, He is my leader, teacher, guide, protector, and provider. Being my best friend, He is my comforter, my voice of reason, my listening ear, my shoulder to cry on, and my closest companion. To me, He truly is a friend that is closer than a brother. I know He wants to be those things for you, as well.

No sugar-coating: the grieving process is a tough and lonely road. Some say it's one of the worst things to go through in life. The lonely silence is often overwhelming, the companionship you once had with someone, the safe place, the best friend you thought would always be there, is no longer there. The feeling of being loved by someone is gone. The countless text messages you got throughout the day from your lover and life partner disappear. Even more devastating: knowing all that is going to someone else now. It's overwhelming knowing that the person who promised you a life of togetherness hated being with you so much that they were willing to give up everything you had built together, just to get away from you. They counted the cost of leaving, the tens of thousands of dollars per year in child support or alimony, the breakup of an immediate family, time away from their children, the loss of friends and ex-loved ones - and, yet, *it was still worth it for them to leave.*

Those are all thoughts and emotions that I had no choice but to go through when I was alone, night after night, month after month. Still, if I hadn't gone through them - and instead moved on right away because I couldn't deal with it all - those thoughts would have just crept up somewhere else in life in a different way.

I struggled with these thoughts (and many others) for a long time. Because someone no longer wanted me, how could I be wanted by anyone else? What do I have left to offer now, that would be good enough? It takes a lot of God and a lot of time to feel whole again. It doesn't *take someone else,* even though you might think so. I've learned to surrender these terrible feelings, as well as my struggle with loneliness, to God. It's all I can do now to get over the oppressive silence, and I never thought I'd be here two and a half years after my separation: still very single. Yet, here I am.

Many people don't talk about this process because they don't stay single long enough to go through it all. If they do stay single, they fill their schedules to the brim with things to do, people to see, places to go - all so they don't have to deal with their issues. (*Of course, I'm not saying don't plan to do anything while you are healing. Having fun and spending time with others helps the healing process; just be sure to have some quiet alone time so you can process and heal properly.*) Once you've settled into a routine of being alone, find one or two really close friends to really pour your heart out to; their feedback and support will help immensely.

I still have my bad days, but most days are good. Some days (every hour, it seems), I still have to surrender my loneliness to Him. Sometimes it takes everything in me not to be overwhelmed with hopelessness about finding my forever-person, and while I'm mostly content with where I am in life, it's still a struggle. I'm beyond thankful that God has brought me from that first place and grateful for the path ahead. I would never be where I am today - spiritually or emotionally - if none of this had happened and I didn't make the choice to deal with it, head-on. I realize that I am so much stronger than I ever gave myself credit for!

Night after night, I sit in my beautiful living room that I've worked hard to make just the way I want. I spend most nights praying, reading, or writing, and God has really revealed Himself to me during these times. I'm slowly learning to rest and be patient, to fully surrender and trust. I'm living in God's goodness like never before. I've been experiencing His peace and learning about His nature - which is amazing. He is naturally loving, caring, so kind, and so generous. Many times, I've been overwhelmed by His goodness and love towards me. I can't even begin to describe how He fills my heart with joy, hope, and *every other good thing.*

One thing I love to do when I'm alone is to crank up my worship music - especially when I'm feeling down. When I'm in total surrender and praise to God, I feel so much better. Praise lifts us above every circumstance and allows God's power to move in us and through us. We do our best spiritual warfare with our praise. Victory comes when we praise. Bill Johnson has stated in many of his messages that we don't fight for victory, we fight *from victory* because Jesus already won the battle for us. He already defeated the enemy. We've already won, and praise allows us to take our victory! Praise also allows us to fully surrender our will to His will, and surrender allows us to see God's loving nature towards us.

Even if your outward circumstances don't change, if you choose to surrender everything to God, praising Him in your storms, you will inwardly grow leaps and bounds. Ephesians 3:20 (NIV) says God "is able to do immeasurably more than all we ask or imagine, according to His power that is at work within us." I believe that covers even the decisions we make in the heat of adversity, according to our faith and trust in God, He'll work it out for our good, no matter what it may look like right now.

Because Jake worked away so much, I had to learn how to live alone early in the marriage. Then, I had to learn it on a *whole new level* once I actually DID live alone! For some reason, I had to get used to people ringing my doorbell at midnight because it happens way more often than you'd think! There's a house the next street over that has the same house number as mine, but I live on 102 avenue, and they live on 102 "A" avenue. This - in itself - is annoying, but making it even more annoying is the fact that none of the people at that house seem to know their own address. I get their mail all the time; it's not the mail carrier's fault, it's their name on it, with my address.

Last summer, I had people come to my door to look at my "basement suite" rental. Four or five different people came for an open house one blissful Saturday afternoon. My kids were yelling and fighting, my baby was crying at my feet, my house was a disaster, and I looked like I was hit by a truck... and I had to answer my door in all this glory. Furthermore, I didn't have a basement suite for rent, the realtor put my address on the advertisement, instead of the house a street over.

Shortly after moving in, my doorbell rang at 1 am. My girls and I were living alone in the house, so naturally, I thought we were all about to be murdered by a guy in a balaclava with a machete. *That's it, then. We're dead.*

Well, it's been fun. Or it could be the police telling me my family is dead. I also considered that it might have been my ex at the door. My heart was pounding so hard and fast you could see my chest heaving. Completely defenceless, I slowly opened the door. It was the pizza delivery man, delivering pizza to the wrong house! A few thoughts came to mind: the first couple, I should not repeat. The third thought was: *If any of my kids wake up now, I'm going to be so mad!* I would never actually say anything (I don't like confrontation), but I considered giving them a really bad review online.

Late-night pizza deliveries happened so often that I finally put a sign on my front door. And, seriously, what kind of job do you have that you don't know your own address - but make enough money to order take out at least twice a week?

Bottom line: on top of surrendering my loneliness, I also had to surrender *living alone,* and trust that God would keep us safe.

Conversations with Sofia

Age: 6

> *Sofia and I are sitting at the kitchen table putting together a Lego set she got for her Birthday.*

> *Sofia - Mom, how long has Lego been around for?*

> *Me - Oh, it's been around forever.*

> *Sofia - So, Jesus invented it?*

Surrendering My Feelings of Hopelessness and Purposelessness

I've been thinking a lot about hopelessness and lack of purpose lately, as both have been a struggle for me for a while. Why am I here? Why am I going through what I'm going through? What is the purpose of it all? Is there any hope that this season will ever be over, or am I stuck in a situationally and geographically cold winter that never seems to end? Can I do something that might take my mind off my current situation, or make it not seem too bad, if even for a short time?

Sometimes I wonder if hopelessness and lack of purpose are huge reasons why people do drugs, drink, cheat on their spouses, commit suicide, or self-sabotage in countless other ways. Perhaps it starts off as boredom or disappointment. Maybe we didn't get the promotion we wanted, and our current position is so boring, it's killing our very soul. Maybe we're disappointed and bored, so we start to dabble in gambling and alcohol. Maybe our marriage is really struggling; we don't know how to revive it because we've already tried and it just feels hopeless, so we start innocently chatting with an old boyfriend from college. Maybe we're just so emotionally and physically tired of the mundane day-to-day of being a parent; and at our children and husband's beck and call, struggling to find our own purpose, so we distract ourselves with a little porn. Maybe we're tackling weight loss, having tried many diets, but it seems like a hopeless cause because nothing has worked, so we try a little cocaine to give us that extra boost. Perhaps we had surgery a couple of months ago, and even though the pain is gone, the memory of how amazing the pain medication felt is still there, so we start taking opioids. Unable to shake the terrible memories from our childhood, no matter how hard we try, we might begin to contemplate suicide.

When we were young, we always dreamt of what we wanted to be when we grew up. And now having grown up, maybe that dream has died, along with any hope of ever accomplishing it. Then, we wonder and question why we're even here. What is our true purpose? Why do we exist? What's the point of doing anything if it's not making a difference?

As Christians, we're supposed to be the ones offering hope and purpose to people, but what if we're struggling to find it ourselves? We're supposed to put all our hope in Jesus, but how do we do that? What does it *look like* to do that?

To overcome these kinds of questions or negative feelings, I - like King David - have to encourage myself in the Lord. I still do it all the time. I read Psalms from The Passion Translation Bible out loud until I feel peace, or until one of the girls screams at me to get them something to eat before they die! Part of being able to surrender completely is learning to completely rest and trust. The apostle Paul encourages many times not only to be content in all situations but always to *have hope and be thankful.* To do that, I spend a significant amount of time thanking God for His many blessings, beginning each prayer time with thanksgiving and praise. Psalms 100:4 (NIV) says to "ENTER His gates with thanksgiving and His courts with praise..."

Every morning on the way to taking my girls to school, we take turns saying what we're thankful for. Depending on our moods, it's harder to find things we're thankful for, but the girls are getting pretty good at it and can usually list quite a few things in a short time. Sometimes it's the trees, the sunshine, or the simple fact there's less traffic that morning. Sofia always says she's thankful for God, Jesus, and the Holy Spirit, our food, and water. I always say I'm thankful for a warm garage to park in, coffee to drink in the morning, and the sunrise (especially in the spring, when the sun finally does start peaking up over the horizon on our way to school). I feel like it changes the whole atmosphere of the car.

I've made myself a list of different attributes of God and things about His nature, and things about Him I'm thankful for, which I will attach after this chapter. I say it out loud almost every day, more than once, if I can. When we shift our focus off ourselves and onto the One who made the entire universe and knows the end from the beginning (and more importantly, loves us with every fibre of His being), our struggles become dim in comparison to Him. Amazingly, when we focus and tell

God how amazing He is, thanking Him for his goodness towards us, we, in turn, feel better. It can take away our depression and give us new hope and purpose.

Thanksgiving and praise have gotten me out of some very despairing and hopeless times, times where I didn't know if I could go on another second. Times when I was overwhelmed by loneliness or frustrated with the girls, or beyond angry with the way things were going in my life. When I praised *through my tears* and was *thankful in my despair*, my outlook and perspective eventually changed.

I Thessalonians 5:16-18 (NIV) says, "Rejoice always, pray continually, give thanks *in* all circumstances; for this is God's will for you in Christ Jesus." That means that in the midst of feeling hopeless or happy, depressed or blessed, whatever you're feeling, whether you want to or not, give thanks and praise. We always seem to want to know what God's will is for us, but it says it right there: *always* rejoice, *always* pray, and *always* be thankful. I guess that would mean that no matter what we are actually doing - whether we are working, raising kids, driving, cleaning, eating, going through a difficult time, you name it - we are still rejoicing, praying and being thankful. Not thankful *for* the hard time, but *in* it. Not thankful *for* the divorce but being thankful *despite* the divorce.

I believe the Lord wanted me to do something else to get rid of this sense of hopelessness: let go of any friends that brought me down. I spend a significant amount of time alone now - which is sometimes hard - but I need to learn how to talk myself back into a hopeful state before I can genuinely and lovingly offer hope to others. They need to be able to see it working in me before they will believe it. I can't tell unbelievers that Jesus is the Prince of Peace if I'm a bundle of anxious nerves and ready to explode at any moment. David had to encourage himself in the Lord, and I've had to do it, too. If I'm honest, I think we've all had to talk ourselves off the proverbial ledge and into a better state of mind when no one else will.

God genuinely loves and cares for everyone. A great way to develop a sense of hope and purpose is to help others by finding something we enjoy doing and then help others do it. Send new moms frozen meals, help dig water wells in third world countries, spend time with lonely seniors, pick up garbage you see lying on the street, or pay for someone's groceries. There's so much we can do to make the world a better place. A small thing I enjoy doing is paying for the coffee for the person behind me in the drive-thru at Tim Horton's. It doesn't cost much and can make a person's day!

Finally, a big way for me to become more hopeful is to focus solely on the good things that are happening. It's very easy to become overwhelmed with all the garbage that's going on in our world, but there are so many good things happening too; we must be diligent in looking for them. Philippians 4:8 says to think on what is true, honest, just, lovely, virtuous, and praiseworthy. What amazing things is God doing in your family? What is He doing in your church or city? He's a miracle-working God, so there is a very good chance that something wonderful is happening somewhere nearby! Has He healed anyone you know? If not, go online and search for other healings. You will find countless testimonies where He's healed people.

Last spring, God woke me up in the middle of the night and asked me if I wanted Him to heal my summer allergies. Since they made every summer so miserable for me, of course, I said yes. Last summer, I didn't have a single symptom all summer long! Amazing, and so much more enjoyable! My favourite part of it all? Those symptoms weren't life-threatening, they just made me uncomfortable, and God cared about me so much that He healed something that small.

I was just at a conference featuring Randy Clark and Bill Johnson not long ago. There were about a thousand people there in total, and almost 200 healings during the whole weekend - it was such a beautiful time!

That weekend, God spoke to me about how He cares about the little things and how His timing is perfect. For example, I've admired and wanted to meet Bill Johnson for a few years now. (His messages have helped me more than he will ever know!) I tried to meet him while I was visiting Bethel Church, but there were so many people...

then, I thought about trying to talk to him during the service at the conference the night before, but again, there were people everywhere.

My mom and I checked into the hotel where the conference was being held. We decided to share a bed and let her cousin, Carol, have her own bed, but when we pulled back the sheets on the first night, there was hair everywhere; yes, so gross! Upon calling the front desk, they came, changed our sheets, and gave us free vouchers for the breakfast buffet - it was very expensive, so we hadn't planned on eating there. The next morning at the buffet, after being seated at our table, my mom suggested we go get our breakfast while she waited at the table. I thought about staying with her but I really needed my morning coffee, so decided to go ahead and fill my plate first. I walked to the "line," (just one fellow in front of me,) and who do you think it was? Yep! Bill Johnson. Heart racing, I started a conversation, chatting for a few minutes and then going our separate ways. My whole weekend was made!

At that moment, God reminded me that He cares about the *little things;* he knew I wanted to meet Mr. Johnson and used something as gross as a hairy bed to make it happen! It was just very cool (heavy, happy sigh). He cares so much about us and gives amazing attention to every detail of our lives. That - in itself - gives me purpose and fills me with hope.

Praise and Aspirations

- Thank You, Father
- I praise You God
- You are so amazing
- Thank You for Your faithfulness
- Thank You for Your kindness
- Thank You for Your love
- Thank You for Your patience
- Thank You for Your goodness
- Thank You for Your mercy
- Thank You for Your grace
- Thank You for Your compassion
- You never fail
- Your timing is perfect
- You love me
- You chose me
- You are so generous
- Thank You for Your peace
- You are all powerful
- You are amazing
- You are marvelous
- You are wonderful
- You are so good to me

- You never let me down
- Your love has no conditions
- You are so wise
- You are my healer
- You are my redeemer
- You are my Prince of Peace
- You are my provider
- You give extravagant gifts
- You are so creative
- I worship You
- You are so compassionate
- Your mercies are new every morning
- Great is Your faithfulness
- You are my best friend
- I love You
- I magnify Your name
- You will never give up on me
- You will never leave me
- You show me what is right and true
- You are my strength
- You give beauty for ashes

- You give oil of joy for mourning
- The joy of the Lord is my strength
- You fill me with hope
- You are my everything
- You keep Your promises
- Thank You for Your promises
- You have amazing plans for me
- You are my faithful Father
- You've blessed me so much
- You are my hope
- You are patient
- You are kind
- I glorify Your name
- You are my help
- You are awesome
- Your love is extravagant
- You are my joy
- You are an amazing teacher
- You are a wonderful counselor
- You are mighty God
- You are everlasting Father
- You know the end from the beginning
- You are the God of miracles

- There is none like You
- You are more than enough for me
- Your spirit is water to my soul
- You are a gentle shepherd
- You are the God of breakthrough
- Thank You for Your healing power
- Your blessings are endless
- Your name is victory
- Your name is beautiful
- Your name is powerful
- Your love for me is endless
- You delight in me
- You're by my side
- You deserve all honour and glory
- You are for me
- You beam with pride when You look at me
- You are truth
- You're on my side
- Thank You that you never change
- Your love is unconditional
- Thank You for Your strength
- You are my rest
- You've defeated death and the grave

- You are my glory
- You lift me up
- You speak to me
- Thank You for Your blessings
- You are my strong tower
- You are always quick to forgive
- You are my safe place
- You are mighty
- You are bigger than anything I face
- You are worthy of all praise
- You've made me clean and pure
- Your word never returns void

- Your promises are true
- Everything You do is perfect
- I trust You
- I surrender all to You
- You've set me free

Feel free to add your own here:

———————————————

———————————————

———————————————

———————————————

———————————————

Conversations with Sofia

Age: 6.5

We're on our way to Five Guys for supper:

Sofia - Mom, I know why they call it Five Guys. Because five guys work there! (Pause, then happy sigh) Wow, my brain is so awesome!

Surrendering My Emotions

When one of my girls gets overly emotional, I struggle to not react out of emotion in return. It seems natural to yell back when someone is yelling at you or feel down when the person who you're with is down - we feed off each other so much. This works with children, and I know my children feed off my emotions if I am cranky or frustrated.

I thought about inserting some interesting brain science at this point, maybe statistics about emotions and then tie it all together with parenting. Then, I remembered that's not the purpose of this book. It's common knowledge that we could all use some help controlling our emotions, especially while parenting. Every child has meltdowns, and most parents struggle with feelings across the spectrum while such meltdowns are taking place (and even more so when it's happening in the middle of the grocery store!)

I'm trying to teach my children about good work ethics, which is often very hard to do because it's usually easier to just do chores myself as opposed to fighting to get them to do it. When I ask Sofia to do a chore, like unloading the dishwasher, she often throws herself on the floor, crying that she has some sort of ailment that prohibits her from doing it: her hip is broken, both her legs are broken (then dramatically drags herself by the arms around the kitchen), her eyes hurt, her neck hurts so much she can barely move. I also hear that she doesn't want to and that it will take her a thousand hours to do it, and she's never doing it again, blah, blah, blah. Once, she apparently stabbed herself with a butter knife and was convinced she couldn't unload the dishwasher because she was going to bleed to death. There was a tiny red mark on her hand, about the size of a pencil tip, but her hand wasn't cut at all - in case you were worried.

When she starts freaking out because she doesn't get her own way, my first instinct isn't something I'm going to put in writing, but I think you know where I'm going with that. It's the same initial feeling that every parent gets when their kids are driving them insane. My second instinct is to respond to her incessant whining, crying, and yelling by... yelling right back. *"Stop your crying or I'm going to give you something to cry about!"* (Mirror, Mirror on the wall, I am my mother after all!)

Reacting out of emotion is something that I've had to surrender to God a lot, and often right in the heat of the moment. When any of my girls react irrationally about something, I want to scream - and I used to, regularly. Slowly, after time, I learned to stop mid-scream, close my eyes, whisper to Jesus that I need His help and His grace right now. Then, I'd try as hard as I could to respond in a reasonable, calm voice. This is likely one of the hardest things I've had to learn. Of course, doing new things that are opposite of what we've always done is always very hard to learn. Purposing to retrain our brain is difficult, *never mind trying to do in the heat of a very emotional moment.*

It's important that when we are in the heat of the moment, we remain aware and open to what the Holy Spirit is saying. Chances are He is trying to tell us to behave differently than how we are currently behaving.

Too often, we respond based on how we are feeling at the time. Shortly after my split with Jake, Olivia accidentally spilled my coffee on the rubber floor mat of my new car. I was already struggling with so many different emotions and was right on the edge that day; I completely lost it in the parking lot of the girls' dance studio. She felt terrible and was so upset that she couldn't finish her lessons. Of my three girls, Olivia feeds off my emotions the most, and I felt awful for acting out like I did that day. I apologized on the way home, and from that point forward, I purposed to try to keep my emotions in better check. This took a long time - and I couldn't do without surrendering my emotions to God *almost every minute.* A few others in my family shared the trait of reacting from an emotional state, and it's not an easy habit to break.

Looking back at my marriage, I was a "Debbie-Downer" a lot. I'm in a much better frame of mind now and in turn find it hard to be around people who are constantly down. There were too many things that used to make me angry at the drop of a hat - from a piece of garbage dropped on our front lawn to someone cutting me off in traffic, I'd become so angry and let it ruin my entire day.

While I still have cranky days, I've learned to surrender those times and feelings to the Lord, and not let my emotions get the best of me. I often crank up the praise and worship music, singing along and saying aloud anything I'm thankful for, or who God is to me; this changes my focus from myself to God.

I've also figured out other tricks to help me get rid of the blues. First and foremost, I try not to even to let my mind begin to entertain any negative thoughts or complaints. If something bad does happen, I set out to find a silver lining in that cloud. We're human, and we'll get down sometimes, but it's important *not to stay there.* As well as looking for a silver lining, I specifically ask myself: *Why am I upset?* I find a quiet place, and for a few minutes, I have a little chat with myself; it may sound silly, but it helps. *"Candice, why are you so upset? What about the situation is making you upset? Is it really that big of a deal? If it is, what can you do to fix it? If not, what can you do to get over it?"*

Often, surrendering my feelings is hard to do. Not long ago, I was in a very cranky mood, nothing was making it better. I was not willing to practice thanksgiving and praise or talk myself out of it because I was so upset. I'm embarrassed to admit it: I was mad because I was so tired of being alone all the time and mad to the point of wanting to die. I thrive on being with people. Spending day after day, month after month, and now, year after year alone - that's been my living nightmare. Throughout the last five years, four of my closest friends have moved away - and the rest of the friends I thought I had are gone. I know this is a season I must go through, but sometimes I go through it kicking and screaming. When one of my girls has a screaming fit, my first instinct is to do whatever I have to make it stop, but that's not what my Heavenly Father did with me while I had this meltdown. I was livid, yet I could still feel Him there, calmly and lovingly waiting for me to finish. And when I paused my thoughts for a second, I could feel Him asking me if I was done. I replied, *"No! I'm furious! This is the worst, and I hate it!"* But even in the midst of this, I could still feel Him there, patiently waiting. After a couple of double stuffed Fudgeeos at 4 am, I calmed down and said, *"Okay, I think I'm done. I'm sorry. What should I do now?"*

"Tell Me how good I am," He replied. I tried to clear my brain as much as possible and fill it with the wonderful things of God, purposely, with my undivided attention, telling Him how wonderful He is, how faithful He is, how good He is, how He loves me, how I trust Him, how I love Him, how His plans for me are good. Somewhere in all that, I peacefully drifted off to sleep. The next morning, out of the blue, a distant friend sent me a very encouraging blog write-up about trusting God on a deeper level; I'm pretty sure it was written for me. One of the scriptures she used in the article was Psalm 37:5 (TPT); "Give God the right to direct your life, and as you trust Him along the way you'll find He pulled it off perfectly!" Once again, my spirit was completely renewed, and I was filled with purpose and strength to keep going - with peace and joy along for the journey. Seriously, God is way too good to me.

And speaking of double stuffed Fudgeeos, I'm pretty sure there are a few left over... excuse me a minute...

SURRENDERING MY CHILDREN

Surrender in Raising My Daughters

We all want what's best for our kids. We want to see them make good choices and do well in life, but also learn to be kind, helpful, and strong in the process. We raise our kids the best we know how to - which can be very different from our next-door neighbour. One person might think I coddle my girls too much, while someone else might think I'm too hard on them. I've had both opinions expressed to me - neither of which I cared or asked for! The only One I seek opinions from is the Holy Spirit.

After my separation, I purposed to make my girls my first priority (after God, of course). I've seen far too many couples split up and rush into new relationships or use other negative coping methods, leaving their kids in the dust to fend for themselves. As much as I was going through heartache, *they were too,* just as much, maybe even more so. Kids don't know how to express themselves, or deal with emotions and grief, and it is our job to try and help them as much as we can. I read books on how to help my girls deal with trauma in healthy ways and I put them in counselling when they wanted it. I tried my best to show them, in tangible ways, that they are loved and my priority, no matter what. I spent countless hours with the girls cuddling on the couch, playing Lego, colouring, doing homework, taking them to dance, talking to them about everything. I do what I can to make my house a place where they (or anyone else, for that matter) can always feel like they are safe and comfortable; a place that's secure and consistent. Olivia and Sofia co-slept with me for a few years after, and despite people's opinion about co-sleeping, they needed me at night as much as I needed them. They would often wake up in the middle of the night with bad dreams, so they'd snuggle up to me, falling asleep while I prayed with them and gently rubbed their back or face. While weaning them off has been difficult, I wouldn't do it differently if given the chance. It's hard to get everything right while parenting through the first few years of separation, and as much as I would have liked to jump into another relationship to forget the last one, I'm glad God saw to it that I didn't date anyone. He knew my kids needed my full and undivided attention during that time.

My oldest daughter, Olivia, turned nine this last spring (2019). I feel like I gave birth to her, blinked, and now here we are. She always tells me that she's my favourite daughter, to which I say, "You're all my favourite, so there!" She loves to be right, so we jokingly argue about that for a solid 20 minutes, every time. She's the kind of girl that I was intimidated by in high school: super smart, naturally athletic, musical, tall, and beautiful. Yes, one of those! She can outrun, out plank, and beat almost every boy in her class in arm-wrestling. Being in ballet and acro dance since she was three and practicing at home all day most days has made her very strong.

She's growing up fast; sometimes, I feel like I'm not handling it well. She doesn't want to hold my hand or hug me in public (sound familiar?) and I didn't realize how heartbreaking that would be! She wants to post videos of herself on YouTube and TikTok doing her acro dance, and I still want her to sit at the table and colour with me.

What is it about the second child? They can sure give parents a run for their money! Sofia is six, amazing, wonderful, and beautiful in every way. She loves hard, plays hard, cries hard (and often), is overly dramatic about everything, very often insisting that she get her own way. She loves to make friends - the more, the better - hates being alone or bored, and overshares everything, just like her mom (used to). She absolutely will not relent if I say no to something. Heaven forbid I say "maybe later;" she'll ask me about it literally *every minute* until later is now. There's not a child in the world that can make me as angry and as happy in a 30-second time span than my Sofia Evelina.

Tenley just turned three this summer. While I'm not certain how she'll turn out personality-wise, she is *the third child*. She isn't afraid of making her presence known, telling you what she wants or when she wants it (which is something very specific and always *right now*). She talks non-stop and is very bossy. She has piercing blue eyes and the cutest quivering lip when she's about to cry. She'll be joining her sisters at the dance studio this coming September, and I cannot wait! Little girls in their tutus are THE cutest thing ever!

My three girls share a striking resemblance, all fair-skinned with beautiful long blonde hair and blue eyes. If you put their one year old pictures side by side, you wouldn't be able to tell them apart! They don't look quite like either Jake or me. I had pre-eclampsia with all three, so they were all a bit premature. Tenley was my earliest and smallest, born five weeks early at 4 pounds, 8 ounces. Her arms were about as thick as an average man's index finger, and her legs were as thick as a thumb. Her little body fit just perfectly in my little hands. When I think about my girls, my heart just swells and melts – they have become my whole world. Despite their resemblance, their personalities are very different, and I'm constantly learning separate, yet effective techniques to deal with each of them.

I've realized that Sofia is a completely different child when she's at school and dance than when she's at home. There, she works hard and is tough on herself - both traits I didn't realize she had until this last school year. My girls are in a French emersion school, where they learn everything in French. At the beginning of this school year (Sofia's first grade), she was given a book with all the letters and sounds, some words, and a few sentences. I don't know French - and Olivia basically taught herself - so it's like the blind leading the blind when I'm trying to help Sofia. When we first started, I was quite impatient with her and easily frustrated. *"They aren't hard sounds, and we just went over this, how are you not getting this?"*

Reading together every day, I'd think of the episode on *Friends,* when Phoebe tries to teach Joey French; he couldn't put any of the words together properly, and she ends up leaving very frustrated.[8] With Sofia though, as soon as I became impatient, she would

---

[8] *Friends.* Written by David Crane. Directed by Gary Halvorson. Season 10. Episode 13. *The One Where Joey Speaks French* (2004)

immediately start saying she couldn't do it or that she wasn't smart and would want to give up. Even my heavy sighing would turn her off and make her unsure of herself. It was very frustrating, and I didn't know what to do.

One night, in a dream, I felt the Holy Spirit tell me to be more patient while helping her with schoolwork because these preliminary stages in reading and grade-one work sets the tone for the rest of her school days. If her attitude toward school is negative now, I'm going to have a much harder time as she gets older. I woke up so grateful for the advice and the newfound grace He gave with it.

It's still a work in progress for me. Every day I must ask for grace when she struggles, gets distracted, or gets mad and cries because she doesn't want to do it. It's a huge battle to get her to do her homework, chores, brush her hair - *anything* - and I struggle with anger. Holding back tears, I quietly whisper through closed eyes and gritted teeth, *"Jesus, You have to help me with this child. I'm really frustrated, and I don't know what to do. I need Your grace."*

"*Ok, deep breath,*" I say out loud to both of us, "*We can do this; let's just try again.*" By this time, I've calmed down and have some peace. "*Sofia, I know you're so smart, and I know you can do this.*" She'll argue with me for a few more minutes, but we eventually get through it. I outwardly praise her for finishing and doing such a good job, while inwardly thanking God not only for His grace, but also because it's over for another day! Now, onto chores, piano and bedtime: more huge battles.

Fast forward six months into the school year: we discover that Sofia can't focus and needs glasses. Thank You, Jesus! We know why there's been such a struggle with reading! Since getting her glasses - *absolutely adorable* - she has improved in leaps academically, and it hasn't been quite as much of a battle.

Recently Sofia was awarded the virtue of self-control at school. I know her teacher knows her well, so I thought this was an interesting award for her. I realize she works very hard in school and must control herself well, but she's a different kid at home: completely over the top, high energy, a crazy amount of feelings all over the place, lots of spills, falls, yelling, crying, and, well... DRAMA.

Still, I make a point of saying positive things about my girls, reminding them of how loved they are by so many people, and 'who' and 'whose' they are. By 'who' they are, I mean they are strong, amazing, kind, brave, smart, beautiful, and so many other things. By 'whose' they are, I mean they are not only mine but also daughters of the most-high King.

Also, I try my hardest not to compare them, realizing that they all have completely different personalities and abilities, so I can't expect them to be as good as each other in all things. For instance, Olivia is naturally good at everything (though timid and shy), while Sofia is the friendliest and most talkative kid you'll ever meet!

Each night when I finally get to bed, I watch them sleep (yes, still in my bed, two-and-a-half years later) and consider how blessed I am to have these amazing girls!

I go through the day thinking about how many times I feel like I messed up: I lost my temper with Sofia for whatever reason. I didn't follow through with this or that. Suppers keep consisting of noodles for days on end because I'm so exhausted, and it's already too late to spend a lot of time making them a dinner they won't eat anyway. Noodles don't provide enough protein and fibre - or much else - that they need. Too often, I let them have too much sugar. When I let them have too much screen time, *that's a whole other chapter in itself!* Sometimes I don't make them brush their teeth before bed because I just don't feel like fighting anymore. I feel like I'm constantly failing as a mother, pouring my heart and soul into these girls, and still, I don't believe it's enough. I should have done *this* more and *that* less.

One day, I was the recipient of unwanted "advice" from a bystander at the store. Tenley was having a typical 2-year-old temper tantrum, and Sofia decided to have a meltdown because she couldn't get a treat. An older lady came up to us, commenting on how beautiful they were. She proceeded to tell me I shouldn't be letting them stand in the cart because it's dangerous, and how parents these days just let their kids scream in public, and how we need to have more control over our kids. *Thanks, lady, I didn't realize that I had no control over my screaming kids at that point. Please, tell me how unfit of a mother I am, that really makes me feel great. And please, tell me how you think I should discipline them. I'll get right on that...*

I think about how I handled it, but also how I *should have handled it*, and guilt sets in. One person undermines me by giving my kids candy after I said they couldn't have any, and another person gets upset at me for letting that happen. It seems that sometimes we just can't win no matter what we do!

Oh, the feelings we feel, the mom-guilt that we put on ourselves, and the mom-shaming we get from others. And if that isn't enough: physical exhaustion. I just returned from attending a social event my parents hosted, where Sofia and Tenley acted up all evening long in front of the entire living room of people, leaving me feeling complete and utter defeat, shame, and embarrassment, just when I thought I had a bit of a handle on things!

"God, for the nine millionth time, I surrender this to You. Whatever this is. My kids, my apparent inability to raise them properly, their behaviour, other people's opinions. Everything. I can't do this alone. I need You. I need Your grace."

The Holy Spirit has been so faithful in helping me raise my girls, providing more grace than I could ever ask for. I think we all struggle to keep our tones positive (and yelling to a minimum) and when I hear my girls yelling at each other, it's clear how mean it sounds. I'm certain it sounds just as mean coming out of my mouth, and children mirror what they see and hear. So many times, I feel the gentle nudge from my loving Heavenly Father, reminding me that, perhaps, I should mirror what I see and hear *when He talks to me:* so much love, patience, encouragement, and grace. This often proves difficult, as I'm called to give mercy when they don't deserve it! I shouldn't enable them to take advantage of me, but right now, it's what the Holy Spirit has asked me to do. So, I say "*yes.*" And suddenly, something in me just switches, my anger turns into compassion and love, and the conversation or argument heads in a more positive direction.

Maybe I can be a good parent. Maybe I was just struggling earlier today. Maybe tomorrow will be better. Maybe I'm not the terrible mom I sometimes think I am. Maybe we, as parents, don't give ourselves enough credit. Maybe we're believing lies from the enemy that we've failed already, so what's the point of trying? Maybe we just need to remind ourselves that we're doing our best, and then surrender the rest to the Lord. He gave us our children, so obviously He thinks we can take care of them. And He doesn't expect us to be perfect, by any means. Maybe He just wants us to surrender ourselves and our children completely and wholeheartedly to Him.

Conversations with Olivia

Age: 9

> *Olivia - Mom, did you take the 20-dollar bill from my wallet?*
>
> *Me - Yes, I did. I'll give it back to you when I get some cash.*
>
> *Olivia - Great, now I won't be able to afford to go to college!*
>
> *Me - What?! Are you serious?!*
>
> *Olivia - Yes! Then I won't be able to get a good job and I'll be homeless forever!*

Surrendering My Daughter's Broken Heart

There's a big beautiful church in Los Angeles called Angelus Temple. There is quite a bit of rich history in this old building, having withstood numerous natural disasters and been a place of relief during the wars. I had the privilege of going to an amazing conference there in February 2018, and what struck me the most about this building was its stained-glass windows: two stories tall, stunningly beautiful, and each carefully depicting a significant moment in Jesus' life.

Shortly after I got home from this trip, Olivia was really struggling with questions about life. "How come I've prayed so much for my mommy and daddy to get back together, and God didn't answer my prayer? What's the point of praying for things if He's not going to answer? Why did God let this happen in the first place? Why do things have to be so hard? Why is my heart so broken?"

I sat there with my eyes closed for a minute, not knowing what to say. *"Jesus, what do I tell my child? How can I* answer her questions when they're the same ones I have?"

But Jesus, being the ever so loving and faithful Father He is, gave me the words and wisdom to answer both of us at the same time. *"Olivia, I want to show you some really cool pictures I took while I was on my trip."* I showed her the pictures I took of the big beautiful stained-glass windows in this large church, zooming in and pointing out all the little details of each window. This was right up her alley, as she is very creative and artistic. She thought they were so pretty.

"Olivia, to make a stained-glass window, you first have to take big pieces of coloured glass, breaking and cutting them into a lot of smaller pieces. Then you take all the different pieces of broken, cut, coloured glass, and fit them together to make a picture. I know you feel like your heart has been broken or cut into a thousand pieces. Mine has too. People make choices, or things happen beyond our control that break our hearts, and sometimes we feel like there's just no way our hearts will ever be the same. And in most cases, they won't. And that's ok, because we can

give the pieces of our broken heart to Jesus, and He will not only carefully pick them all up, He'll also lovingly put them back together in a way that will make the most stunning picture. Anything we give Him, He makes beautiful. I don't know what the future holds for our family, but I do know that no matter what it looks like, it will be wonderful and beautiful, just like these stained-glass windows." I gave her a big hug and kiss, wiped the tears from her eyes, then mine. "*Does that help a bit?*" I asked.

"Yes," she said, "Ok, I'm going to go play now." From then on, every time we went somewhere that had a stained-glass window, she'd point it out to me with a big smile on her face.

I could have never come up with this example on my own. I know it was wisdom from the Holy Spirit. Every time I go back and read this story, my eyes fill with tears and my heart swells with gratitude for such a beautiful way to explain a tough topic, like broken heartedness, to a child in such a way that would not only speak to her creativity but also remind her that things will be okay.

Conversations with Sofia

Age: 4

As I'm putting Sofia to bed one night:

Me - Honey, you look tired.

Sofia - Yeah, I've been working out

Surrendering Social Media and My Children

I think every parent is wondering how much screen time their kids should have. We're all sitting between feeling guilty for letting them have too much screen time and being worried about the potential addiction it may cause, and the desperation to give them something to do so they'll shut up for five minutes. Then, there's the other side where we consider that it's how they do a lot of learning in school (and it's not going **away**), so we might as well let them learn to use it, so they're not left behind. I've entertained all these arguments many, many times. Tenley gets up so early in the morning, and sometimes I give her my phone to watch Netflix, so I can sleep for another 20 minutes. (Don't judge me. If you're a parent, you've likely done it too! If you aren't yet a parent, you *will* do it, no matter how many times you say you won't!)

I used to say that I'd never let my kids misbehave in public, and if they did, they'd quickly learn not to. I also used to judge other parents quite harshly, but then I had kids of my own. I took the girls to Walmart when Tenley was a baby, and she was screaming because she was hungry, Sofia was having an absolute fit because I wouldn't buy her a toy she wanted, and Olivia was angry that she couldn't have candy. One of the managers gave me a sympathetic look and opened another till so I could quickly pay for my things and leave; that was greatly appreciated! I learned the hard way that we need to be there for others, helping each other out - whether we know them or not. We shouldn't judge - or be judged by others - about our parenting skills. We're all learning as we go.

I try not to give Tenley my phone to play with too often, but at times it makes more sense to let her have it than to listen to her scream for an entire eye appointment, like she did two weeks ago. Sofia asks for my phone a lot because if she's not constantly entertained, she gets bored. While I used to give it to her more often, now that she's a bit older I'm encouraging her to find other things to do. I want all my children to become creative, but sometimes it presents a challenge going from constantly being entertained to having to make your own entertainment.

What do we do if our kids are on social media sites, being bullied, convinced they are losers, should harm themselves, or being stalked by sick men who are trying to get them to send inappropriate pictures? When I was young, my parents encouraged me to listen to Christian music exclusively because everything else is bad. Not too long ago, my conversation with my six and eight-year-old went like this: *"When you're online and someone tells you that you should commit suicide or harm yourself, or they want to see pictures of you, you need to come tell me right away!"* These are parent conversations today; this is what we are up against - and worse. So much has changed from when I was young, and I find it hard to keep up.

There are 12-year-old twins that live down the street from us, and they used to come over last summer just to hang out with the girls. They are very sweet and polite. One of them has a YouTube channel, and they thought it would be fun to do a live video at my house with my girls. I didn't think much of it until I overheard them say, "Oh, my goodness, someone just commented and wants to see our belly buttons!"

I was up those stairs in record time, trying to keep my composure, but inwardly freaking out. I didn't think I'd have to have the internet safety talk already, but apparently it was time. I sent the twins home, sat down with my girls, and had a nice long chat about what is and isn't appropriate on the internet. Wanting to see their belly buttons might sound innocent, but it often can - and does - escalate into wanting to see more. And more than likely, it's a dangerous adult behind the other screen asking for it. It seems like every week there's something new to talk about regarding internet and social media - and I don't even have teenagers yet! I told the girls they could make YouTube videos as long as they weren't live ones. To me, live videos are more dangerous. They had a hard time following that direction, so I deleted our account. They can still watch it on their tablets, they just can't post anything. When Olivia discovered TikTok, I set boundaries as to what kind of videos she could post. And when she went against my word, I deleted that too. Olivia now says she's the ONLY ONE in her class that doesn't have TikTok, EVERYONE else has it except her. I reminded her that perhaps she should have respected the boundaries I set.

While it may seem like a simple solution, the option of taking away cellphones, tablets, and laptops won't work either. Our kids have access to social media or YouTube in many different places they go - even most televisions are "smart" now - so they can watch anything they want or chat with anyone they want; trying to take that away is likely to cause a rebellion.

Because of a sleeping curse, Sleeping Beauty was forbidden from touching any spinning wheel for fear for her safety. Spinning wheels were banned in the kingdom, but if she had just been taught how to use them safely from early childhood, perhaps she wouldn't have let her curiosity get the best of her later in her teenage years!

I believe that's also how we should approach our kids with social media and screen time. Since we can't forbid them to use it completely, we should teach them what is appropriate, what is safe, what is okay, and what is not okay. Teach them not to type things that they wouldn't say to a person's face and encourage them to be kind to others online. Tell them that if there's anything that ever makes them feel uncomfortable, they can and should talk to an adult about it right away. Teach them common sense about not believing everything they read and hear on the internet. Teach them to take breaks from social media. Offer to play games and do other activities with them as alternatives. Be involved as much as you can.

Off and on over the last few months, my girls have been afraid of the dark and going to bed because they believe some hacker will come into the house and hurt us. Not too long ago, they were afraid of the "Momo" creature that all the kids in school were talking about. It ended up being a hoax but still gave Olivia bad dreams for a few weeks after. I tell both Olivia and Sofia that no bad guys of any sort are allowed in our house because Jesus is protecting us and will not let anyone or anything bad inside. I tell them that Jesus already beat all the bad guys when He died on the cross and rose again for us, so we don't need to fear. Because He is in our hearts, we have the power to tell any bad thoughts to get out of our mind, in Jesus' name! And since Jesus is the Prince of Peace, we can ask Him to give us peace and help us think only good thoughts, and He will! We still must purpose in our mind to think only good thoughts, but He will help us do it.

I also limit their tablet time, suggesting many other things that are more important - like homework and being active and creative - so, those take pre-eminence over their tablets.

Last year, God made it clear to me to limit Olivia's tablet and phone use because it was stifling her creativity. I must be very intentional about this because it's so much easier to let it go rather than encouraging her to be "creative" (making messes!) When I was visiting Bethel Church in Redding earlier this year, three different times people were praying for me and all of them, in different ways, had a word of knowledge about my girls and I being creative, and learning how to express it. I didn't pay much attention at first because I was hoping to hear words of knowledge about *my future*, but since then, I've sat down and prayed about different ways to encourage my girls to show their creativity, the first part of which involves *getting them off of their tablets;* the second part involves spending a lot of money on craft supplies and being okay with the huge mess they'll make!

For the most part, Jake and I agree with each other in parenting and are pretty good co-parents. But since he's made the choice to walk away from the Lord, his values have changed. I don't like the girls listening to inappropriate songs, but he doesn't care. He lets them get away with more in areas like that, and probably always will. They come home from his house and play me a new hit song - which is not for children's ears - but I hear them singing along. Great. It's difficult knowing that when they're at his place with his girlfriend, and talking about God, church, or the values at my house, her kids tell them that those are stupid and make fun of them. When my girls say they aren't allowed to watch a certain TV show or types of YouTube videos, they're met with more sneers and comments. I worry about how I'll convince them to keep these values and still live for Jesus when they're teenagers, because I remember being a teenager and compromising my faith here and there *just so I'd fit in.*

I've struggled with this, having to seriously commit and surrender it to the Lord continually. Clearly, every Christian parent wants their children to grow up loving the Lord, doing everything we know to do, yet our kids can rebel. It seems even more difficult when the father of the children isn't serving God.

I try not to worry about it because, eventually, there will be nothing I can do - aside from praying and being there - for my children as they grow up and make their own choices. When I do pray for them - which is continually - I tell the Lord that they are His, and I surrender them to Him. I've asked God to give me specific things to pray for with each of them, and He's been faithful to that, so I've been faithful to pray specifically for those things. I pray for Olivia's heart, I pray for wisdom for Sofia, and I pray for Tenley's destiny. I pray confidently because I know the victory is already mine. I thank God for His promises to me, like His promise of keeping my girls safe and healthy. I do my part and teach them how to be safe on the internet, while crossing the street, etc., but then I commit them to Him and let Him take care of the rest.

And I stand in faith in those promises, knowing that whatever the future holds, God has His hand on them.

The Holy Spirit is such an amazing covering over my girls and for myself. I have such great conversations with them about all aspects of life, and I believe that they understand. I try always to have an open door and no-judgement policy; I hope it still works when they are teenagers! I'm always praying for them, throughout the whole day and often during the night, and I'm quick to apologize to them if I've said something I shouldn't have, or if I've used an angry tone with them. I express my concerns about them being online or listening to inappropriate music, always trying to give reasons that make sense to them. I'm vulnerable and real with them in a way that they can relate to and understand, but without guilt or condemnation.

I believe it is very important to plead the blood of Jesus over our kids. Through His death and resurrection, He bought and paid for our peace, healing, and salvation. His blood covers it all. He defeated death, hell, and the enemy. We give those things way more credit than they ever deserve, and once we are saved by the blood of Jesus, they no longer have power or authority over us. But we must submit our wills to Jesus and follow His leading and guidance. We must stand in the gap for ourselves and our children and plead the blood of Jesus over them and us. *Every day.*

I consider my children to be amazing gifts from God... most of the time. Sometimes I'd like to return them, but apparently, they're non-refundable. In all honesty, they are treasures that I often don't I feel like deserve, so every day I do the best I can to raise them and show how much I love them. Every day I ask for the Holy Spirit's guidance, strength, and grace to be the best mom I can be. When we feel like we're not enough, He picks up our slack and does what we can't. I gladly surrender my girls to Him.

Surrendering Not Knowing How My Girls Are

When my girls go to their dad's house, I try my best not to worry about them. He's a good dad, fairly hands-on, and makes sure they are well taken care of. I realize that's more than a lot of other single moms can say about their children's dad; I'm grateful.

Though it sometimes feels like I don't know *where* they are (they go to other homes for sleepovers, parties, and such), my biggest concern is *how* they are. Perhaps I overthink it, but my girls are still young, and I want them to know that if they have a bad dream, they don't have to be afraid. Or if they feel unsafe somewhere, they know what to do or how to leave that situation.

Things are different for them, depending on where they are. For instance, if they have a bad dream at their dad's house, they tend to be left dealing with it on their own; at my house, they get in bed with me, are cuddled, and prayed with. Breaking the habit of them being able to crawl in bed with me at will has been harder than I thought - especially with Sofia. I haven't been able to break it, maybe because I feel guilty that I'm not there for them *all the time*, so when I am there, I overcompensate. Or perhaps I fear that their dad is doing it right - making them figure out how to deal with things on their own - and that they won't need me anymore.

As I write this chapter, its summertime (2019) and the girls are on holidays in interior British Columbia, with Jake, his girlfriend and her whole family. In other words, my girls are staying with a bunch of people I don't know. Since they just Face-Timed me to tell me all about their adventures, and though it's hot there, I know they are getting sunblock put on them twice a day, are wearing hats, and having a great time. *What I don't know about* are the sleeping arrangements, and it bothers me that I'm not there to take care of them if they have bad dreams or get scared. What if someone is mean to them? Worse: what if it doesn't get dealt with? Men tend to under exaggerate and disregard feelings, so if there is an issue, are my girls' feelings being ignored? On the flip side, women tend to over-exaggerate and dwell on feelings; am I overthinking all of this, worrying about nothing?

I've had to surrender this issue many times over the last few years. I can't be there for my girls all the time - and it's very difficult for me - so, I've tried teaching them that even though I can't always be there, Jesus is always there. He always cares. He'll always give them peace and take away their bad dreams, if they ask Him. And even if outward situations don't change, He will always help them deal with any inward feelings and issues they have.

The girls still struggle with our divorce - they don't like having to leave one parent to go to another. And they're right: it's hard, and I don't like it either. They want mom and dad to get back together and for us to be a family, but it's not happening. We've started doing birthday parties together, but I think that'll be as far as it will ever go. Still, it breaks my heart that my girls are still so grief-stricken about it. But God is still so good, still providing peace that passes all understanding in the middle of our brokenness and chaos.

"*Again, Lord, I surrender my kids to You. I ask that You keep them safe, wherever they are. I ask that You give them a good rest tonight, and good dreams. Give them peace, Father, and a reassurance that You'll always be there for them, no matter what. Remind them that they are Your daughters and they can come to You whenever they're afraid, unsure, or any other thing they go through. I trust that You will take care of the precious treasures You've given me.*"

Conversations with Sofia

Age: 7

> *Sofia - Mom, remember you promised me you'd take me to Florida, just the two of us?*
>
> *Me - Yes, honey. I will. As soon as I win the lottery, we will go to Florida. (wink)*
>
> *Sofia - Well, did you buy a ticket?!*

Surrendering My Miscarriages

Miscarriage almost seems like a forbidden subject. It's a hard subject, sure, but also such an important one to be open about. Countless women have had at least one, and we need to be there for each other during such difficult times.

I've had three miscarriages. My first one was between Olivia and Sofia, at 11 weeks - just enough time to be very sick for the first trimester, and then it was over. At Christmastime.

My second and third miscarriages were close together, right before I got pregnant with Tenley. The second one was at 6 weeks, right after we had told everyone we were expecting. My third miscarriage was the most traumatizing one, at 19 weeks. When I told Olivia that the baby in my tummy went up to heaven, she said "Oh no! Not again!"

It was both a traumatic and devastating experience. I went to the emergency room because I was spotting, but

I didn't think too much of it since I was past the first trimester. I went in to be on the safe side, but when they did a quick Doppler Ultrasound, they were unable to find a heartbeat - or even an image of the baby. I fought hard to not have a meltdown in the middle of the room. The next morning, I went in for an emergency ultrasound; the baby was measuring at 13 1/2 weeks, so I had lost it quite a while before. My OB doctor had me come in at eight weeks, then said I didn't need to come in again until 20 weeks. At the time, I thought that was odd - in light of my history - but I complied without protest. Had I trusted my gut, I'd had gone in earlier, and learned of the miscarriage sooner. As it stood, I wasn't *technically* at the half-way point of the pregnancy, so I couldn't "deliver" at the hospital. Instead, I was given a prescription to take at home; it would contract my uterus and expel its contents. Jake tried to pick up the prescription for me, but the pharmacist insisted that I come personally, explain it all, and sign a consent form. That afternoon, his parents took the girls for the weekend; we stayed home to have a baby. It was a sad, hard day.

We gathered the remains of our baby, unable to tell its gender, and took it to my parent's acreage, where my dad made a tiny little coffin. Jake and my brother dug a hole in the woods, and we laid our child to rest.

Miscarriage is very rarely someone's fault. It's hard not to want to blame ourselves for it, but we never should. There are always so many questions: Why did it happen? Did I do something to cause it to happen? Could I have done something differently to prevent it from happening? Is there something wrong with me or my body? I remember breaking down while in the shower, uncontrollably sobbing, wondering if I lost this baby because I sometimes drank more than one cup of coffee a day. The simple truth is that pregnancy is hard and risky for anyone. Even with all the medical advances we have now, there's still never a guarantee of anything. We can be as healthy as humanly possible, and it still might not work out. Or we may not be healthy at all, and the baby can be just fine. One just never knows.

Even now, years later, my mind still sometimes wonders why I lost those babies. I find myself a bit angry because they're gone, and I don't know why. But as soon as those feelings come up, I pray and surrender them all to the Lord. It's not beneficial for anyone to stay in a place of anger or resentment, especially about things we can't control.

The most comforting thing to know is that even if we're unsure, Jesus knows. He cares and loves us. Again, I don't know why He lets some things happen, but I do know He causes everything to work together for our good. Even the ugly, devastating things in our lives.

In 2013, God promised me another baby. At the time, I was content with the two I already had. But He knew I needed Tenley, long before I even knew. It was a long, painful process to get her, but she was - and is - worth every second of it.

(I've written this as Tenley is currently at the most developed stage of the "Terrible Twos," and I'm hoping to still believe it when she's 15...)

SURRENDERING MY PHYSICAL BODY

Surrendering My Self-Image - and My Girls' Self-Image

For years I struggled with insecurity and self-image. I constantly beat myself up about things regarding my body, my skin, hair, wardrobe, my personal style, my lack of motivation to work out. You name it, I struggled with it, constantly comparing myself to other women.

One of my sisters just recently had a baby. After six weeks, she was immediately on the elliptical, working out every day and eating healthy. I worked out with her, lasting two days. She is so motivated to work out, and she's very self-disciplined in terms of money-management. Yet, she is very stylish and can make anything look good, including sweatpants. She sits out in the sun for one day and has a beautiful, perfect tan. She's so funny, yet quiet and private with her personal life. I used to compare myself to her often.

My former sister-in-law is - in my mind - absolutely stunning. She's part Cree, so she has the perfect, natural almond skin colour. She's tall and beautiful, stylish in everything she wears. We went to New York a couple years ago, and she literally turned heads everywhere we went. She also has this quiet wisdom and grace about her, as if she knows exactly who God made her to be, and she's not afraid to step into that. She totally rocks at being a mom of four young kids! I used to be so intimidated by her, always comparing myself to her.

Jake's girlfriend is everything that I thought I wasn't. She is tall and in great shape. She enjoys running, which I'd rather die than do. She has a very good paying job, is smart, fun, adventurous, and stylish. Plus, she is a fantastic stepmom to my girls. At first, I was bitter about all her great attributes, but in time, I've learned that she's a wonderful woman, and much better suited for Jake than I ever was. Still, I couldn't help comparing myself to her at the beginning.

There should come a point in every person's life where they can look at themselves in the mirror and see how wonderfully made they are, and how loved and cherished by the Father they are. How much they have to offer the world. How valued and worthy they are - and not because of what someone does or doesn't say. They discover and start to love who they are because they know *Whose they are.*

If that day hasn't yet come for you, I hope and pray it comes soon. Though I don't remember the exact day, I do remember standing in front of my full-length mirror criticizing and comparing, wondering what was so wrong with me that I wasn't wanted. Out of nowhere the Lord spoke to me and said, "You know, Jake left Me too. And I'm God. He didn't just walk away from you for whatever reason you think, He walked away from Me too. And there is absolutely nothing wrong with Me. I created the universe. I'm God." Then He reminded me of how loved and cherished I was by Him. It was a beautiful and intimate moment that I'll never forget. Since then, I've often had to surrender my insecurities to the Lord, but before that moment, I didn't even see that as an option.

Every time I have a moment of insecurity, in one way or another, He always reminds me how beautiful, loved, cherished, and valued I am.

It was then that I started to see myself differently, and genuinely love myself and love my body for what it looked like then - and what it looks like now. I'm 5'1", and my feet are so flat that I can't wear heels, even if my life depended on it. I have thunder thighs and a ghetto booty that would look great if I had the willpower to do squats or lunges every day; sadly, I'd rather do anything else in the world than to work out and eat healthy! I've been pregnant six times all together, so I have a bit of a belly, but all the desserts and lattes I enjoy certainly don't help! I can rock leggings and a casual T-shirt with a hoodie - like no one's business! My hair looks pretty decent when it's down but drives me crazy sitting on the back of my neck, so it's usually in a messy bun. I don't look like any of the women I described before, but I'm okay with that now. They're all beautiful in a tall-bombshell type of way. I am beautiful in a cute, fun type of way, which matches my personality. I am who God created me to be. I don't want to be anyone else, and I don't want to *look* like anyone else. We can always adopt different clothes, make up, and hair styles from other women, but we shouldn't want to *be* them.

Learning to love myself is something that I'm working hard to pass on to my girls. I watch Tenley look at herself in the mirror, so happy, smiling at herself and saying "I tootie" (cutie). I watch my two older daughters look at themselves in the mirror and criticize. Olivia says she has dark circles under her eyes and isn't skinny enough. From where - and at what age - did they learn all that? Of course, that's a rhetorical question; they learn it at early ages and from anywhere and everywhere. I've heard Sofia say her legs are too fat, all because someone called her a "big fat tattletale." I know the other kid didn't mean that she was literally fat, but why is it so natural for us to take something like that out of context in such a negative way?

I recently met someone whose daughter is in the hospital fighting anorexia. I didn't understand any of it, so I boldly asked her what a day looks like for her and her daughter. Wow - were my eyes ever opened! To have to sit with your child and listen to them say how much they hate themselves and want to die, and there's absolutely nothing you can say or do to make them believe otherwise. To try and force them to eat, but they're petrified of getting fat, so they refuse to the point where they eventually end up on life support. If they DO eat, they can't be anywhere close to a sink or toilet or they'll make themselves throw up. If she doesn't happen to be in the room with her daughter, she often gets phone calls from the nurses, any time, day or night, asking her to come because her daughter is curled up in the fetal position on the floor, banging her head against the wall, or cutting herself. As she shared her awful reality with me, it was hard to hold it together because I was so sad for her and her beautiful daughter. Then my mind zeroed in on my own daughters.

It's amazing how powerful the mind is; it's even more amazing how we can train it to do or *not do* certain things. My new friend has had to purposefully train her brain to turn off thinking about her daughter at certain times of the day so she can function in her life and deal with her other children. She told me she had to learn to do that, or her anorexic daughter's situation would have destroyed her, as well. I've had to purpose to train my brain to think more positively about everything - including the new fear of my girls struggling with anorexia, or me struggling with my self-image. When I say, "think more positively," I mean *completely surrender it to the Lord.*

I make it a point not to criticize myself in front of them, if at all. I've even started saying good things about myself, which is new for me. We can tell our children how beautiful, handsome, or wonderful they are all we want, but if they see or hear us criticize ourselves, it cancels out anything positive we've ever told them. In their mind, if we say we are ugly, and they come from us, then that must mean they're ugly too. I also try and correct anyone when they say something like, "I can't lift you, you're too heavy." *No, she's not too heavy, she's perfect just the way she is.* To say someone is "too" something or "not enough" something implies just that: they're not good enough and need to be "less" or "more" of something. A better way to say it would be, "Wow, you're growing up so fast!"

My biggest goal in life (other than to raise my daughters to love the Lord) is to raise them to love themselves in such a way that they're strong, they know who they are, what they believe, and what they want out of life. I want them to be unafraid to stand up for what is right, to be strong against negative peer pressure because they know their truth: they are completely and lavishly loved by their Heavenly Father and are amazing daughters of the most high King. I believe that when we know Whose we rightfully are, then we aren't afraid to be who we really are. To even attempt to do this, I constantly need to stay covered under the Holy Spirit, continually seeking His guidance and wisdom, and being willing to do whatever He tells me to do.

I don't want my girls to see me falling for any guy that pays attention or tells me I'm pretty. I want them to see that I have standards, almost impossible standards that the Lord asked me to have because He believes I'm worth it. And when God decides the time is right, He'll bring the right guy along, a man who is everything I need and want, and nothing less, and who will love me for me. I'll have so much to offer him because I already know my value. (Ladies, you don't need a man to remind you how amazing you are. If your self-worth is based on a man's opinion, you'll be constantly disappointed and hurt).

Conversations with Sofia

Age: Almost 4

> *Sofia - Mom, you're, seriously, the greatest mom!*

> *Me - Thanks, honey, how come?*

> *Sofia - Well, sometimes you let me do stuff.*

Surrendering My Low Energy Level

I believe the enemy attacks each one of us in different ways. When God calls us to do something, the enemy will use whatever he knows we struggle with, so we don't accomplish our purpose. I've always struggled with is a lack of energy and am especially drained and tired when I'm feeling down about something. Oddly, I also feel drained when God puts me in a new exciting season and fills me with purpose. Sometimes it feels like I'm losing the battle.

A couple months after having Tenley, the girls and I moved into a new house, and I found myself raising three small kids alone. Tenley was awake every 45 minutes to an hour during the night for the first six months. She'd finally fall asleep for a longer period of time around 6 am, but by 7:30 am, the alarm would ring, and I had to get Olivia ready for school and out the door.

Looking back, I know it was only God who gave me enough energy to get through six months of sleepless nights, having to function fully throughout each day, all the while dealing with the emotions of separation. I am beyond thankful for that. I know there were many times during the last eight years prior, that I would sleep a full night and still be too tired to function in the day. I remember times when Olivia and Sofia were little, just the thought of giving them a bath was exhausting!

I know God has really helped me a lot in this area, and I've learned to ask Him for strength just to do daily tasks. I've also learned that the joy of the Lord is my strength, so I'm determined to create or choose joy. The easiest way to do that is remaining thankful. I've looked for the silver lining in every cloud. I've been grateful for things like sweatpants and warm hoodies, socks, and slippers. I've been thankful for things like the beautiful sunrise. I say out loud things I'm thankful for. *"Thank you, Jesus, for coffee. Thank you, Jesus, for loving me. Thank you, Jesus, for my warm house and a garage to park in."* When I was especially down or tired, I started writing out attributes of God and worshipful sayings in Psalms, as well as things I was thankful for. Before I knew it, I had written pages and pages!

When I was transitioning into my new season of writing, I battled (and still do) with fatigue. I feel an urgency to write this book, but at the same time, all I want to do is sleep. When I don't have my girls, I have to go to a coffee shop to write so I don't even have the option of choosing to sleep over writing. When I do have my girls, I'm busy most of the day, but in the evenings, I'll purposely have a cup of coffee, so I stay awake long enough to write something. This is a battle I must bring to God often because only He can give me the strength I need. Jesus and coffee have always been - and will always continue to be - a great team and a great help to me!

God has asked me to start living a healthier lifestyle; eating better, drinking more water, being more active - things like that. I find it very difficult because I've never been one to turn down a dessert or initiate a workout. In fact, I've often skipped supper just so I could eat more dessert. While it may sound awful, I'd rather just not eat anything for a few days to lose weight instead of going to the gym. Clearly, I have a very, very long way to go and am going to need a ton of help from the Lord to get my butt in gear, literally.

What I don't need, though, is unsolicited exercise or diet advice, or motivation from others who are trying to recruit. When any of my social media friends begin a new training regimen, start drinking energy shakes, take on new diet fads - anything of that nature - and need three more friends to sign up, I almost immediately unfollow them. I refuse to work out or do a fitness class with anyone because it brings back memories of my junior high, high school, and university days when we had to do group exercises - and I'd get laughed at. I suppose I should surrender this too. Ugh.

Surrendering Diet Pills

This is a tough topic for me to write about. I thought about adding this to my last chapter because it's somewhat similar, but I feel this is an important issue of its own. I've lost quite a bit of weight over the last almost three years, and I'd rather people *not know* that the last year of weight loss is owed mostly to a pill. It's hard to share that if I didn't take that pill daily, I couldn't function without being completely exhausted or eating everything in sight. I liked that it gave me energy, helped me to lose weight without doing much exercise, and I wasn't famished all the time. I liked that people were commenting on how great I looked, but I didn't like feeling like I needed the pill to survive.

Shortly after I had Tenley, I was still swollen from pre-eclampsia and weighed about 165 pounds - not the healthiest weight at 5'1". The combination of stress and not eating - both caused by the separation - brought my weight down to about 130. With the addition of diet pills last year, I lost another 15 pounds. Clearly, none of these methods for losing weight are good or healthy, and

144

I don't recommend them. No one can function on little to no food for any length of time, and though the pills kept me from FEELING hungry (so I didn't eat), they also gave me a sort of fake energy, so I didn't feel like I needed to eat or sleep to function. My body was in starvation mode, and it was only a matter of time before something bad happened; I knew I had to start making better choices.

For months after the Lord asked me to lay those pills down, I fought with Him about it. *"What if I stop taking them and then can't stop eating? What if I'm exhausted and can't be a good mom because I need to sleep all the time? No, Lord, I like how things are going, so I'll just continue taking it. I'm sure it's fine."* When lying in bed at night - after resting for hours - I'd notice that my heart was still racing - really racing. *"Well this can't be good."* I googled "racing pulse", finding many explanations; none were good. *"Ok, I really need to start taking better care of myself. I must stop taking these pills. I'll do it the next time the girls are at their dads, so I have some time to ween myself off."*

Once I had prayed about it, surrendering it to the Lord, when the box was empty, I just stopped taking them. The first day I simply forgot to take one until lunchtime, but I knew it was too late in the day to take one, or I'd be up all night long. So, I just didn't. Prior to this, if I'd forgotten to take a pill, I'd need at least two naps during the day, I'd have to be in bed by 8 pm, and would feel like death all day long. But this time was different. I felt okay. I wasn't as tired or as hungry as I thought I'd be - which was fortunate, because I had not waited for the girls to go to their dad's before quitting the pills. I still had to be a good parent. The first week went well, but the second week, I ate pretty much everything in sight!

Oh, the terrible things we put our bodies through for the sake of appearance! I'm thankful that God cares about us so much and that He wants us to be healthy. But, of course, He should want that! Perpetually unhealthy people are ineffective in the works of the Kingdom. Their bodies can't handle it. And why should they? If we're required to be good stewards of our money, time, family, church, then we should also be good stewards of our bodies, as well.

I've gained a bit of weight back, but I'm slowly learning how to take better care of myself and eat healthy. I'm not dependant on any diet pills anymore. Still, getting healthy the right way is going to be a long learning process, and I must be intentional about it every day. My mindset about weight and a healthy lifestyle is something I'm going to have to surrender to the Lord on a regular basis.

***It's now been six months (it's March, 2020 (this book is taking forever to write and edit!)) since I stopped taking these diet pills, and I wanted to write an honest update about how this has been going: not well. Granted, I haven't touched a diet pill once, but I've gained 25 pounds in six short months. I was addicted to sugar and I couldn't get enough. I was napping two to three times a day and had no energy for anything. Knowing this wasn't normal, but also not knowing what to do, I just let it happen. Thankfully, God was still prodding me to get healthy, and actually gave me a dream of what my next step should be.

I went to see a wellness specialist two weeks ago, and got bloodwork done. After looking at the results, he was shocked and wondered how I could function on a daily basis. My vitamin B12 is low, my thyroid (T4 and T3) is low, my iron is low, my vitamin D is low, and my blood cells are very small and aren't able to carry enough oxygen to my entire body. My body is coming out of starvation mode and storing everything as fat, and my muscle mass is extremely low. On top of all that, my estrogen and progesterone levels are also low. Not the greatest of news, but at this point it's all still fixable, and I'm glad I have answers now. I'm not entirely blaming the diet pills, because I've never had much energy, but I do know they made it much, much worse. (Please, PLEASE learn from my mistake and don't take diet pills of any sort! They are so terrible for you!)

So I'm now starting to take the appropriate measures to get healthy. I'm taking the proper medication to get all my levels up to where they should be. I asked the Lord to give me the desire to eat better, and He did. My sugar cravings drastically lowered, and my desire for vegetables and fruit is slowly escalating. I'm trying to eat clean; more whole wheats and less processed foods. I know this is going to a long, hard road, but if I want to be around for a while, it needs to be done.

Conversations with Sofia

Age: Almost 5

> *Sept, 2017 - Sofia had her introduction to Kindergarten; it only lasted two hours. When I picked her up, she came out of the class so happy, and said so excitedly:*

> *MOM, I DIDN'T EVEN HAVE TO GO TO THE OFFICE ONE TIME TODAY!*

> *LOL, good for you Sofia. (The mom standing beside me almost fell on the floor from laughter.)*

SURRENDER AND TRUST

Surrendering Money, No Job, No Education

A huge aspect of being a single parent revolves around money. I know of many women whose husbands have left them and refused to pay any child support; that's illegal, and I'm not sure not sure how they get away with it. I also know of women whose husbands have left and the women have taken them for everything they have; I don't agree with that, either.

When Jake and I split, we owned three houses and two vehicles. We handled things pretty well in that we each kept our own vehicles, each kept a house, and we sold the third house to pay off joint debt. Since he has a well-paying job, I receive a comfortable amount in child support. So far he's never withheld child support, and I've never tried to get more out of him. I'm sure the thought has entered both of our minds at some point, though. If either one of us has a rough month, we try and help each other out. I appreciate that he does what he can to make sure we are taken care of financially; I know a lot of single moms who cannot say that.

Even so, I have felt pressure from everywhere to get a job or start some sort of training/schooling for a career. I know things won't always be the way they are now, and I know should something ever happen to Jake, I have three kids to support, and will need some sort of income by my own means. Sometimes God asks us *not* to do things - like working, in my case - and trust Him instead. Personally, I believe it might be easier to trust myself to get a job or career to generate income, as opposed to not working and having to wait and trust the Lord for my finances and other needs. That stance doesn't make sense. He created the whole universe and everything in it, He owns the cattle on a thousand hills, as Psalms 50:10 says, and He has access to everything. So, why is it so hard to trust? Perhaps because it's hard to constantly live in the unknown. We know who holds tomorrow, but it's scary when we don't know what tomorrow looks like. For me, guilt plays a part. I feel like I should be working, but instead, I enjoy my day with my toddler, and spend as much time as I possibly can writing, praying, reading the Word or other books, and worshipping. Most of my time is spent growing in my relationship with my heavenly Father.

Every once and a while, the guilt sneaks up on me and I begin thinking that I should be contributing financially. There's no reason why I shouldn't be working. I go back and forth wondering what kind of job I could do with the little to no formal training I have. Then I think, *"Wow, Candice, you are 34 years old and have absolutely no skillset of any kind. Good for you. You're going to go far in life."* Before I know it, I'm neck-deep in shame, regret, guilt, inadequacy... the list goes on. My pity parties have gotten shorter and fewer because I've learned what to do in these times: Surrender. Praise. Worship. Ask God what He wants me to do.

The answer is always the same: Wait. Trust Me. Rest. At these times, I feel His kindness and goodness so strongly. He gently asks me "I've taken care of you and provided for you all this time; do you think I'd stop now?"

"No," I sheepishly reply, *"but I just feel bad. I feel like I'm doing nothing."*

153

"You're in a position where you can spend countless hours a day with Me," He replies, "that's all I want from you right now. You. You know I will always take care of your needs and wants. I love taking care of My children, just like you love taking care of yours."

I think of my girls, how much I love them, and how I would do anything to provide them with what they need and want. I think of the time I spend with each one of them individually, and how much I cherish it, never wanting it to end. I have to smile when I realize how much joy my girls bring me and am reminded again how God's children bring Him joy. I can feel Him smiling at me with loving, tender affection, and I'm in complete peace. Nothing outward has changed, but, once again, my soul is transformed.

I've learned to trust God with my needs. I don't feel like I'm supposed to work at this moment; I feel led to write. For a very long time, I felt that I was supposed to simply wait. Do nothing, just wait. That was difficult, because I'm very "administrative" and like seeing things get done. It's a different season for me right now, and every season will be different for you. You may be working, or not. You may be a stay-at-home mom, or not. You may have a lot of money or extra time, or not. One thing always should be the same: we must put God first and foremost in every aspect of life, *trusting Him completely*. In our abundance or lack, whichever it is, seeking God for every provision or seeking God to possibly give away any extra, He is first. Always.

Sometimes, God asks me to give away money, perhaps its extra money I've been saving for a trip or a new pair of jeans. Other times, its money that I really need to pay bills with and buy groceries. He even leads me to take money from my credit card and give it away! At times, it's not a great deal of money, but at other times, *it is.* I used to talk myself out of giving away the money God asked me to, but then I'd feel convicted, asking for another chance to obey. Since He's the God of a million chances, He'd always give me one, but it seemed it was always when I was least expecting it - and at the *least opportune time.*

When I was 20, I started attending Trinity Western University in Langley, British Columbia. The year prior, I had worked hard as a restaurant server, saving up for my first year of school, and I always had cash from tips. Countless times, the Lord asked me to put the cash in my wallet into the offering plate at church - even above and beyond the tithes I had already given. Admittedly, I started emptying my wallet before leaving for church. After all, I was trying to save up for college, and I couldn't save anything if I was giving it all away!

The Lord had other plans and was trying to teach me to trust Him and His provisions. During my first year at TWU, the last payment for the year was due and I had no clue how I was going to pay it. Many of my friends knew I needed money for the rest of my tuition, and I know they were watching to see what would happen. "She keeps saying that God will provide," they thought, "but will He really? Does He care that much?" Sure enough, at the last possible second, God came through and there was an extra $3000 in my bank account to pay for school. At the time, I had no idea how it got there; I was blown away by His love for me.

I love giving money away - it's so fun! Don't get me wrong, sometimes I'd rather put it on my credit card or buy a new Kate Spade bag to add to my collection, but it's always encouraging and a blessing to watch Him take my two fish and five loaves, bless it, and feed thousands with it.

Surrender During My Weekend at Bethel

Not long ago I went to visit a friend who is attending the Bethel School of Supernatural Ministry in Redding, CA. I had been frustrated and discouraged, needing a change of scenery, and since the girls were with their dad for a few days, I decided to go. (If you ever get a chance to go to Bethel Church, do it - you won't regret it!) Before I left on the trip, a few people jokingly mentioned that maybe I'd meet a nice guy while I was down there. *"Yeah right,"* I thought, *"like someone would possibly ever love me enough to leave beautiful California, move up to where I live (where dreams freeze to death), and take on me and my three children."* Deep down, that's exactly what I hoped would happen; I didn't expect it, but I hoped. I tried many times to surrender those thoughts to God, but it was fun imagining what meeting him would be like.

We'd both be at the Friday night service, because, well, I would have to leave Sunday and we'd need time to get to know each other. We'd lock eyes and, surprisingly, I wouldn't look away - his piercing baby blues wouldn't let me. He'd smile the most beautiful shy smile I'd ever seen, my knees would buckle, and I'd run out of air. I'd try and smile back, but I'm sure I'd look ridiculous. It wouldn't matter though; a spotlight and big flashing arrow pointing on him from heaven would immediately settle all questions and insecurities. During the entire service, I wouldn't be able to concentrate. I'd try to steal as many glances at him as I could without making it obvious to everyone around me. He'd catch me every time and we'd smile. After the service was over, he'd timidly walk up to me and introduce himself. Despite him and I locking eyes so many times, he would turn out to be quite shy. Obviously, he'd have to know how insanely gorgeous he was, but still, he would have a genuine meekness and kindness about him. The friend I was visiting would be an acquaintance of his and would already know that he was a high-quality guy.

He'd be a doctor, obviously, with either a British or Australian accent, because either one is so attractive! He would be on a sabbatical, spending a year at Bethel, trying to figure out where God was leading him. Enter: me. He was already thinking about moving to Canada anyway, so this was perfect! He always wanted kids, but he wasn't sure he could have any. He had been married before, having a similar story to mine.

His ex-wife sure taught him how to dress well; not in ridiculously skinny jeans that no man should ever wear, but straight-leg, dark denim, and all the other stylish clothes men wear. He was definitely a guy's guy, *and I needed him in my life as soon as possible.*

But, of course, I've surrendered all these musings to God... as you can tell. And - as God would have it - none of that even remotely happened on my trip. The first night there, I was so distracted by these thoughts that I couldn't pay attention to the speaker. I had to surrender these ideas almost every three minutes or so! It turned out of be a fantastic trip, and I left there so spiritually full and loved on by the Father, which was good - I needed all that for the trip home - when I realized I lost my passport.

The trip home was a prime example of when God says to trust Him, we still need to keep an open mind to all possible outcomes - and even outcomes that seem impossible. After a long drive Sunday night from

Redding to San Francisco, I had checked in to my hotel, and was about to check into my flight when I realized I couldn't find my passport anywhere. I searched every pocket and piece of clothing in my suitcase and backpack three times, realizing that I hadn't *actually seen* my passport all weekend. After about an hour of searching (and intermittently freaking out and praying frantically), I felt the Lord tell me to just trust Him and go to sleep. *"Ok, deep breath, trusting Him. He probably means I left it at the airport, so it still must be there. Ok God, I trust You."* I said those three words *"I trust You"* over and over, all night long. *"Surely God wouldn't let this wonderful weekend end in such a negative way. Him wanting me to trust obviously means I'll get it back from the airline tomorrow and be right on time for my flight. Perfect."*

It turns out that's not what God meant at all. My passport was nowhere in San Francisco. I sat in the airport sobbing like the scared, broken-hearted little girl I was. For the next 45 minutes, my conversation to God went something like this: *"God, how could You do this to me? You told me to trust You and I did. I trusted that You*

161

had it here and everything would be okay. But it's not. So now what do I do?"

Meanwhile, I had been texting a friend about everything; he turned out to be a total Godsend. He advised me to call the Canadian Consulate who, in turn, advised me to fly to Seattle and drive across the border to Vancouver, then fly home from there. Ok, I could do that. I booked the next flight to Seattle, and in the security line, I once again expressed my frustration to the Lord. I had cried off all my makeup, and probably looked like I had been hit by a train! *"Well God, this isn't how I wanted this weekend to end."*

"I know," He said, "but do you still trust me?"

I took a deep breath, *"Yes, I do still trust You."*

I could feel Him smile at me with the gentlest, loving eyes and say, "Am I still good?"

I smiled back, *"Yes, You're still so, so good."*

Fast forward to an extremely delayed flight in San Francisco, a snow storm in Seattle, an expensive hotel, a long drive in an extremely expensive rental car through a storm and the border (which - thankfully - was a *lot less hassle* than what I was expecting), two more extremely expensive flights, many, many conversations between God and I... and I was home! My passport was found (no idea how that happened) and I was able to pick it up in Vancouver on the way home. Things worked out, as they always do when God's hand is in it.

Conversations with Sofia

Age: 4

>*Me - Sofia, go brush your teeth please.*

>*Sofia - But my hands can't work the toothpaste!*

>*Me - Yes, they can.*

>*Sofia - But my hands don't know how! They just can't take it anymore!*

Surrendering My Dream (or Lack Thereof)

When I was in high school, my dream was to become a wife and mom. Since I was six, I wanted to have a little girl and name her Olivia. The dream came true; I did become a wife and a mom, not only to an amazing little girl named Olivia, but two more wonderful little girls. Being a mom is a lot harder than I thought it would be, but it's still incredible. Being a wife wasn't as much fun.

I've since realized that even though motherhood is very important - and what I'm meant to do for right now - God has plans for me that are outside of that. In prayer, I've told the Lord that I don't know what I want to do with my life, and I don't have a dream, and that thought depresses me. I felt Him say, "That's because what I have planned for you is bigger than anything you could ever dream for yourself." I thought maybe I'd be the next Lisa Bevere or Christine Caine, but only God really knows. And I'll be happy with whatever He has planned.

The problem is: *"what's my next step? Where do I go from here?"*

He said, "Forward."

"Yeah, but which way is forward? What does that mean? What do I do? What's the plan?"

"Just put one foot in front of the other."

"In what direction?"

"Forward."

"Ugh, sometimes God, You're really frustrating."

"Yep. So you are just going to have to trust me then, aren't you?"

Exasperated and frustrated because I know He's right, I throw my hands in the air. *"Fine."* Sometimes I'm so glad my neighbours can't see in my window because they'd think I was crazy.

These are some of the conversations I've had with God - not joking. He wants us to be real, honest, and vulnerable with Him. He's okay with us talking to Him like we would talk to our best friend, because that's what

He wants to be for us. I've prayed many prayers regarding my future, my dream - or in this case, lack thereof. Countless times I've expressed my frustration because I don't have a passion for anything and don't feel like I contribute to society, other than raising my girls. Don't get me wrong; it's such an important job and I'm not diminishing it in any way, but all of us have a special calling on our life. I was so determined to find mine; I didn't realize that if I seek God's heart instead, that calling *will find me.*

I feel that God has called me to write. Though I've already been writing this book for the last few months, I think it may be more than just a one-time thing. While I have no idea what that might look like - even within the next year (never mind, the next five years) - I've been slowly learning to throw my hands in the air and let God take care of it all. So, as much as I can today, I'll spend time with my heavenly Father, and I'll write. And tomorrow, I'll do the same. Some days I'll write a lot, and some days I won't because my children's activities are my priority that day.

Whatever I do, I want it to align with God's heart. That's *all I want*: to be obedient to whatever He's asked me to do. Whether He says go or wait, I'll do it. The outcome doesn't matter, because if I'm obedient on the journey - no matter how hard or long - it will always work out.

If God has given you a dream, go for it passionately trusting that He'll guide you along the way. If He hasn't given you one, but instead has asked you to trust Him step-by-step into the unknown, trust Him, putting one foot in front of the other. It's not easy, but it's oh-so-worth-it!

Ever since we were little kids, we were taught the scripture, "Trust in the Lord with all your heart and lean not on your own understanding. In all your ways, acknowledge Him and He shall direct your paths" (Proverbs 3:5(NKJV)). A while ago, the Lord brought me back to that verse and asked me to put it into practice. As time went on, He'd ask me to do things that didn't make sense, like give money away that I really could have used. Then He'd ask me to trust Him for the provision that I needed. A couple times He asked me not to date certain guys, even though it made sense in my mind to date them (more on this later).

Now, I like to apply the second part of the verse *first*. In all my ways, or everything I do, I try to acknowledge Him, or ask what He thinks I should do about a certain situation. Then, even though it may not make sense to me at all, I still try and trust Him completely and be obedient. I've failed many times, but He always kindly and mercifully picks me back up, helping me to get going again.

Conversations with Sofia

Age: 4

> *Mommy, you're the cutest mommy ever! You're just so cute, I could cry!*

Surrendering My Time

I like a clean and organized house, so much so that my girls and I would spend most Saturdays cleaning everything instead of enjoying fun times together. Olivia sometimes scrolled through my Instagram page, commenting on how everyone else was doing fun things - and all we did was clean. Not entirely true, but also not the way I want my kids to remember their childhood. It's a bit of a struggle because a messy house gets me emotionally down and overwhelmed. And with three young kids, it's easy for it to become a mess really quickly, and hard to keep it at least tidy. If you're a parent, you know the struggle!

I am also a bit overly concerned with little things - like how the pillows are placed on my couch or how my couch, chair, and area rug all have to be in perfect line with the grooves in my hardwood floor, and evenly spaced from each other. (The blanket placement on my book cover absolutely kills me.) I hate clutter anywhere. My cabinet in my dining room must be equally spaced between the two side walls, and I like my kitchen table to be perfectly centered with my cabinet, also in line with the hardwood grooves.

I think I became more consumed with a clean and organized house because there are so many huge areas of my life that I can't control, and this is one I can. I thrive on getting things done; when I feel overwhelmed with anything and everything, I can at least calm myself down and say, *"Okay, what's one thing you can do? Clean the house. Okay, where should you start? In the living room. One room at a time... you got this. You're going to be okay."*

Because I am a one-woman team - and because the Lord specifically asked me to spend more time with Him - I've had to let some things go. Obsession with a clean house was one of those things. I thought that listening to a message or worship music while cleaning would be good enough. While that's great - and still very important - it wasn't what He meant for me at the time. As parents, we learn to multitask very well, very quickly. I could worship, clean and organize the house, bake, make lunch, organize my day, all at the same time, like no one's business. But God wanted my time, *undivided*. There were things He wanted to share with me that He could only do so if I was completely resting in Him, yielded to His presence.

Three months ago, my dishwasher leaked all over my kitchen floor. The hardwood was destroyed and had to be taken out. The same hardwood runs throughout my whole main floor; it can't be colour-matched, so it must all be replaced. For the last three months, my kitchen floor has been blue plastic taped over plywood. My cabinets were taken out and are still sitting sideways, and my island is being held up - somewhat - by 2 x 4s. Everything that was in my cabinets and island are now all in boxes lined along my dining room wall. While my disdain for doing dishes is high, at least I have a kitchen sink in which to do them, but since my sink is in my island (and they have to replace my whole island), it's going to take even longer to get it remade. Bottom line: I'll be hand-washing dishes for the foreseeable future. It's utter chaos on my main floor, and all I can do right now - besides waiting for insurance to go through and for it all to be fixed - is to walk around it all and make sure my kids don't hurt themselves. Perhaps God's lesson involved removing the only thing I thought was keeping me sane (cleanliness / orderliness) and keeping it that way for months so I could learn to let it go. When it rains, it pours, right?

I've been learning that in the midst of chaos, I need peace. When God asked for my undivided attention, I knew it was something I had to do. I gladly give back ten percent of my gross increase as tithes to God, but He specifically asked for ten percent of *my time*. I wasn't sure what He meant: ten percent of my awake time, or ten percent of the entire day? Immediately, I knew the answer. Ten percent of a full day is two and a half hours. That's a lot of time. I've been realizing that all people in effective ministry spend a lot of their undivided time with God. Most days I can do it, but it was something I had to work up to - and I can't do it every day. Sometimes, I sit for hours, praying, reading, and writing. I'm trying to release my grip on what state of order my house is in - God doesn't care about that - He cares about the *state of my heart*. When He has something to tell me, I want my heart to be completely open and free to listen and receive.

Tenley goes to a day home Tuesdays and Thursdays, and I spend as much of that time as possible with the Lord. Those times are precious!

I seem to get easily distracted (which I'll elaborate on later), so a while ago I decided to get up early in the morning so the Lord and I could spend time together. The first day was fine, like it is when a person decides to start a routine. The second day was not as good; I'm pretty sure I fought sleep the entire time. By the third day, I was sound asleep in my living room chair when my alarm went off to get the kids up for school. *Great, this is obviously not working.* I tried to keep going for a few more weeks. Some days were good, other days, not so good. Then, for some reason, I stopped getting up in the morning and decided to spend my entire Tuesdays and Thursdays, while Tenley was at the day home, doing devotions and writing. I had to stop scheduling appointments and coffee dates during that time, focusing exclusively on my priorities. I knew God gave me free time so we could spend it together. He's so faithful. Even though I have poor time management skills, He still made a way for us to be together. I didn't have to do other things during those quiet days, so I finally stopped making excuses and hunkered down with Him.

I also think the Lord meets us where we're at, working with our weaknesses, giving us strategies and new methods of doing things when we're struggling with something. Time-management was a challenge for me because two hours could go by and all I'd have done during that time was scroll social media and stare off into space, thinking about everything and nothing - all at the same time. Before I knew it, it was noon and I had accomplished nothing all morning! So, He's been working with me to be more conscious of how I'm spending my time. Even if I have only ten minutes before I must do something else, He reminds me that I could offer up a short prayer. Again, this is another thing we must choose to be intentional about; eventually, it becomes second nature, but until then, we have to *purpose to properly manage our time*. And whatever we need help with, we can surrender it to Him, trusting that He'll help us.

I couldn't find the perfect time of day to spend it with the Lord; sometimes mornings worked better, sometimes the afternoon, either before or after my precious nap. Because I have small children who go to bed early, the evenings often worked best. Still, every day I tried to be intentional about getting time in, whenever I could. Importantly, I didn't beat myself up about it if I didn't find the time to sit in my chair and spend hours in prayer or devotion. Moms are busy and I know God understands that. He's okay with us talking to Him as we drive all over town, running from school to piano to dance to gymnastics. He's fine with us talking to Him as we're getting groceries, gas, or just running errands. It has become second nature for me to talk to Him all the time, constantly asking Him what He thinks about things or thanking Him for whatever - and I love it.

The cool thing about God is that once we have learned to surrender our time, He can redeem what time was lost. He can make situations happen so fast that it's as if time was never lost in the first place! I have a fun story about how He redeemed quite a bit of my lost time - I'll share it later in the book.

SURRENDERING OUTSIDE INFLUENCES

Surrendering Distractions from Everywhere

I'd like to say that I'm consistent with my time with God, but I'm not. I must be intentional every day. My time with the Lord varies from day to day, every day, week and month is so different. Sometimes, I do so well, other times, I'm so distracted, I can barely get five minutes of alone time. As a busy mom, this is what my day sometimes looks like, and I think many other moms - or anyone for that matter - can relate:

6:00 am, my alarm goes off. *"Ugh, I hate mornings. Girls don't have to be up for another hour and a half, but Tenley will be up in less than an hour. I should get up and do devotions. Ugh, I don't want to... maybe I'll just pray while I'm laying here. Good morning God. I love you and all, but mornings are hard, so let's just hang out here. Okay? Okay. Thank you for being so awesome and wonderful. Thank you for everything you've..."* I'm asleep.

6:29 am, Tenley barges into my room and starts screaming for my phone. *"Here, take it and be quiet. Dang, I missed my devotion time. I could start now, but it's hard to do over Paw Patrol. I'm just going to try and sleep for another half hour and do devotions later. What Tenley? You want milk? Okay, stop whining, I'll get up and get it for you. Ugh, I hate mornings."*

Sitting down to read the Bible out loud while Tenley is awake: Psalm 37 (TPT):

Make God the utmost delight and pleasure of your life... *"What do need, honey? You want Paw Patrol on? Ok, one second, just let me find the remote. Where did you put the remote? I can't find it anywhere... oh here it is, upstairs in my room, that's great. Okay, let me put on Paw Patrol for you. Oh, you don't want that anymore? What do you want then? You want Boss Baby? Okay, one second... You don't want that now? Well honey, do you want Boss Baby or Paw Patrol? Paw Patrol? Okay, I'm turning it on, you can't change your mind now."*

...and He will provide for you what you desire the most... *"Just a minute, I'll get you some apples in a second... Stop*

whining! Okay, I'm getting them now for you, hold on! ...
You want the peelings off?! They're already all sliced!
Okay, stop screaming, I'll peel each one. Here! You better
eat these!"

...Give God the right to direct your life... *"What now? You
want milk? You just had water! Okay, stop screaming,
you can have some milk! You don't need a cup with a lid,
the cup you're using is fine. Just be careful you don't...
and you spilled your milk everywhere. Great. Sure, I'd
love to clean that all up. Okay, sit here at the table and
eat your apples and drink your milk quietly! You're going
to wake up Sofia and Olivia if you keep crying!"*

...and as you trust Him along the way, you'll find He
pulled it off perfectly... *"No, you don't need bread with
Nutella, eat your apples! Okay, okay! Relax! I'll get you
a piece of Nutella bread! Yes, I'll cut off the crusts. Here!
Now be quiet and eat!"*

...Quiet your heart in His presence and pray; keep hope
alive as you long for God to come through for you. *"Ugh,
do you really need a blanket while you're eating? No, you
don't. You can have one when you're done eating and*

sitting on the couch. You're done eating now?! You've hardly eaten anything! Sigh...okay, here, sit on the couch and you can have the white blanket. You want the blue blanket? Seriously, kid, you're driving me crazy. Maybe I'll just read later. Oh, what's happening on Instagram..."

However, sitting down to do devotions when Tenley is at the day home? *Okay, I have six hours to do a ton of reading and writing. Awesome!*

Mom texts: "You want to meet later for coffee?"

"Yeah sure, I'm doing devotions this morning, so maybe after lunch?"

"I was going to go to Costco around lunch and grab a few things. Maybe have a quick bite to eat there too with your dad. Do you need anything from there?"

"Actually yeah, I need some bread and coffee cream. Ok, I'll meet you there at 11:30."

Me to myself: *Okay, I'll read and pray for an hour and then shower, get ready and go to Costco and then go for* coffee… dang, that's almost a whole day… I'll just do more devotions tonight… I should check Facebook real quick…

Finally, some alone time. Tired, heavy sigh. *"Thank You Father for everything. Thank You that You are so good, faithful and kind. Thank You for this day, as frustrating as it was. I pray Lord, that You'd give me patience with my girls. Help me to… Wow, my area rug needs to be vacuumed. And what is that spot right there? Is that the chocolate milk Sofia spilled the other day? I thought she cleaned it up! Yes, because a six-year-old knows how to properly clean up a large spill. Right. Where was I that I didn't help her? I'm kind of getting tired of this carpet anyway, I wonder if that nice one that I liked at HomeSense is still there. When did I see it there? Maybe it was back around Christmas time. Oh, it's probably gone by now. I hope this next Christmas is better than last Christmas. Not that the last one was bad, but I'm just excited for something different. There will be a new baby at Christmas, so that'll be fun. Awe, I'm so excited Alisha and Drew get their little girl! Having one of each will be so fun for them! I wonder how Brixten will do with a little* sister, I'm sure he'll love her. He's such a good little boy. Him and Tenley are going to have so much fun this summer. They're a bit older now so they can be a bit more independent in the back yard and at the park. I'm so excited and ready for warmer weather. Taking the girls to the park is something I want to do way more this summer, for sure. I hope it's hot, but not too hot. I hate wearing shorts. I should really start doing more squats now... Facebook had this great article on working out, I wonder where it is... (45 mins of scrolling later): Oh yeah, Thank You Lord..."

I'm not proud to say that many of my days look like this. Still. Even after I've learned how important it is to always put God first in everything. We get trapped in our complacency, not knowing what to do to get out of it and are often too complacent to do anything about it. This is similar to how I know what sugar does to my body, I know that I feel awful after I've had too much of it, but I still have too much of it - way more often than I should. Sometimes I can go for a few days or weeks of consistently spending time with the Lord, feeling great emotionally and spiritually, on cloud nine. Then, something in life distracts me, our time together dwindles down, the relationship begins to suffer, and I feel like there's a bit of a wall that I've put up. God never puts up walls between Himself and His kids; that's always all our doing. I know what I need to do to fix it - and I want to - but I don't have the drive that puts my butt in gear to get back on track with God. Distractions come from anywhere and everywhere, robbing me of any and all time that I could (and should be) spending with God.

Throughout this book, I've kept you up-to-date of things I'm doing and challenges I'm facing as I write, and so far it's taken me seven months to get here, going through all sorts of different situations and emotions in the process. Right now, I'd say that distractions are a huge issue for me. Part of it is my kids, but mostly it's because I've let other things take priority over God, and it both hurts and frustrates me deeply; I say that nothing is more important than Him, but my actions sometimes don't reflect that.

My heartfelt prayer is this: *"Lord, I am sorry for being so apathetic and complacent. I don't want to stay in this mindset for another second. I ask, Father, that You would give me wisdom and help me discern between what things are actual things that need to get done during the day, and which things are mere distractions. I ask for strength to let those distractions go. I want You to be my number one priority in every area of my life. Help me to seek first Your kingdom and Your righteousness. I love You so much and I want my life to always reflect that."*

Conversations with Sofia

Age: 4

> *Me - Sofia, where did you put the baby wipe container?*
>
> *Sofia - I set it right on the table and it disappeared! Maybe God took it!*

Surrendering My Church

This is a hard topic to write about because my church is so small, and I'm so closely involved with everything that happens there, as well as the people who attend. My mom and dad are the pastors, and we've been attending this church since before I was born. I love how tight-knit we are and feel like many of the families are *my family*. I have my Lay Minister license, serve on the leadership teams, and sometimes fill in as a speaker for my mom. Speaking is probably my favourite part of it all; I don't think I'd ever have that opportunity anywhere else. I really love our little body of believers.

Being so heavily involved and closely connected to the leadership in both a small or large church can make things difficult for people or relationships. When you know what is going on behind the scenes, or are a part of making administrative decisions, it's very important to be aware of the environment in its entirety. In a small church, it's difficult to have the freedom to do things (like sleep in and miss church on Sunday) without everyone knowing about it, and asking why you weren't there.

187

Even harder to do that when you're in a leadership position without some having an opinion about it.

Where our church is concerned, the biggest thing I've had to surrender to the Lord (aside from the possibility of going elsewhere to meet more people), is how to make our church grow, and not just in numbers, but in terms of helping current attendees, myself included, desire to grow spiritually or get passionately excited for God. Or even how to get us all to church on time!

I think most of our congregation has gone through such hard times as of late, and it's been difficult for people to just hang in there. I also think that's happening everywhere. I believe God is allowing us all to go through a season of hard times (wildernesses) because He's preparing us for greatness, and we need to be ready for all that it entails.

I often think of the Apostle Peter, one of Jesus' closest friends during His ministry. When Jesus was crucified, Peter denied even knowing Him, three times; thus reaching his ultimate low. Still, it had to happen for Peter to become completely broken and surrendered to

188

God. Jesus knew that Peter would do that, and as much as it hurt Him, our Saviour knew it was necessary. It truly breaks the Father's heart to see His children so broken, but He knows it's crucial for us to go through, to be able to be fully committed to Him and completely surrendered to His will. I strongly believe that's what many people in our congregations are going through right now. Sometimes it's all we can do to just open our eyes and get out of bed on a Sunday morning, never mind getting dressed decently, kids ready (and not fighting with each other), on time, and "shouting the victory," praying for and encouraging others, all at the same time.

My mind travels back to Peter. Following the ultimate lowest time of his life - once he really submitted himself - he became effective in his ministry. This encourages me. It just goes to show that God doesn't care what you've done in the past, all He wants is you to completely give Him your heart, *in however many pieces it's in.* If we truly understand how much He unconditionally loves us and only wants what is best for us, God's church would be an unstoppable force. We'd quit fighting and bickering amongst ourselves about petty theological issues, getting out into the world, and loving everyone in it, as Christ loves us, giving His life for us all. It's fitting that I think of Peter in all of this because Jesus - knowing what Peter would do and did do - gave him the name "Rock," prophesying that He'd build His church through him and the gates of hell would not prevail against it! Take that scripture and use it as a weapon against the enemy! Satan cannot have my church, nor any of the people, in it because our foundation is Christ, who's already defeated the enemy. None of his schemes or attacks will prevail against a unified body of believers, completely surrendered and empowered to do the work of the Lord!

But still, my church is tiny. The chances of me meeting someone new and handsome who loves Jesus and sweeps me off my feet is close to 0.1 percent. Luckily, God usually works best with those odds, so we'll see. I've asked Him if He'd release me to attend somewhere larger with more people, but He's always said no. He not only wants me to stay here, but He also wants me to serve in whatever ways I'm needed, expecting nothing in return.

"Alrighty, then. To be honest, I'd rather not, but if You want me to, I will. I guess I'll just not meet new people and be alone forever... No, no, it's fine. Being alone is fine. I've gone to this church my whole life and never had a Christian friend my age, so it's not like I'm not used to it. I'll stay here, at my little church, do my jobs here, it's fine. I'm fine..."

Those feelings, above, are real and honest. Sometimes we feel on top of the world with Jesus on Sunday and then complain about how terrible life is on Monday. That's called "life." We all have highs and lows. The important thing to realize is that it's not wise to make big decisions while you're in your lows. If the church you're attending isn't what you thought it would be, if someone offended you, or if you're disappointed about the size of the congregation, don't decide to leave right away. Surrender your feelings to God. Genuinely share with Him legitimately how you feel, because he genuinely cares! Once you do that, ask Him what you should do. Don't act rashly until you've heard from Him - which may take a while. Hang tough, no matter where you are. Then, when He speaks, be open to what He says.

Chances are, He'll say something you don't want to hear, but if you're completely surrendered to Him and His will, you'll be obedient, no matter what it is or how you feel about it.

Surrendering Friends (or Lack Thereof)

To be completely honest: I'm kind of jealous of women who have friends. I have a few acquaintances, but no true friends who make me a priority. Even more honestly, I think a lot of women don't have many - or any - friends. I think many of us spend a lot of time alone. If you do have a best friend or a few close friends, be thankful and don't take them for granted.

To my fellow women with no friends, how do we put ourselves out there? Where can we go to meet new people? It's so hard to make that first step and not only put yourself out there, but then invite another woman to coffee or a playdate, and then follow through. Yes, it's uncomfortable and awkward, and we may not know what to say, but we should still do it, for our own benefit. I really need to start putting myself out there more. Ugh, even just the thought scares me a bit.

I've lived in the same city for the last 30 years, so I should have a well-established friend circle, but I don't. I've narrowed it down to the top two reasons:

1) My personality - I'm sometimes a know-it-all, and moody, I often overshare, say something stupid, and talk a lot. I used to be judgemental and self-righteous, I'm probably very annoying, and I wear pyjama pants too often. But who isn't any - or all - of these things, sometimes?

2) I'm hoping this is actually the reason. God is taking me to a different place in life, and I need to go through a season of loneliness to become better prepared for my next season. I've said before that I used to ask other people's opinions about things *before* I'd ever ask God. And God is making it so that He is my only option. He wants to be my confidant, my best friend, my lover, my provider, my healer, my comforter, my protector, my everything.

I've had to learn to surrender my loneliness and lack of friends to God. I know He cares, but I also know He knows what is best for me at this time. I wish I knew the reasons for everything that's been going on in my life, or how it all pans out in the next couple of years. Quality time is my main love language,[9] so I've always practiced the other love languages just so I could spend time with people I care about. For instance, I might make a dessert just so people will come over and visit. I absolutely love spending quality time with the Lord, and I can definitely feel when I haven't spent as much time with Him as I should. Still, I miss companionship with people my own age.

Growing up in a small church didn't help. When I was 13, someone my age finally started coming to my church. Together we started checking out other youth groups around town. It was fun - and I met a lot of other people - but after a while, that only tore my friend and me apart. I had friends in school, but their values were different than mine, and that became more and more apparent as we all got older. Everything became different; they started to drink and party, sometimes smoking pot. I had a boyfriend from another school at the time, so all my free time was spent with him. All of that (plus my being a Christian) were factors in why my friends and I

---

[9] www.5lovelanguages.com

stopped hanging out after graduation. I don't regret not participating in their parties and such, but I *do regret* making my boyfriend my top priority. I wish I would have taken more time to find myself and what I wanted out of life instead of catering to his every whim.

Fast forward 15-20 years later: I've just finally found myself. My head is on straight, and I know what I want out of life. One of those things is a best friend, someone who shares my faith, but whom I can be real with. Our kids can play together while we sit and drink coffee, talking about our spouses, life, what we had for supper last night, our struggles, how our relationship with God is going, and everything in between. I need someone to be real with, and them be real with me - with no judgement from either side. I want to be able to go over to their house in my pyjamas - no bra - with disheveled kids in tow, and not be judged from her *because she's in the same state of disarray!*

I recently found an old journal entry I wrote last year. Reading it made me sad all over again:

Believe it or not, I was actually invited out to a friend's birthday dinner! She's a dance mom like me, and we've gotten to know each other over the years. The ladies are all enjoying wine, and I don't drink, mainly for the reason that I don't like the taste of alcohol. Sometimes that makes people uncomfortable, even though I don't care if they drink. One of the girls started telling us a story about how she and her husband of ten years were trying to spice up their love life, and a couple of things they tried. But then she felt the need to apologize to me about the story. I was so confused as to why she thought she needed to do that. Because I am divorced and single? Because I am a Christian? Did she think I thought I was too above that? Or that I wasn't a real person with the same kinds of feelings and desires? Is my self-righteous past coming back to haunt me?

One thing I've learned over the last few years is that I really enjoy hanging out with people who are real and unapologetically themselves. People who are open about their struggles as well as triumphs. I feel like everyone - regardless of beliefs or gender - appreciates authenticity. Sometimes I wonder if the best kind of witness I can be to unbelievers is to be an open and honest person, not afraid to share different aspects of my life, as well as someone who unconditionally loves everyone because I am unconditionally and lavishly loved by my Father in heaven.

Conversations with Sofia

Age: 5

>*Sofia wrote her name in blue permanent marker on my white nightstand, right before bedtime.*
>
>*Me - Sofia, what are markers for?*
>
>*Sofia - Paper.*
>
>*Me - So, tomorrow, you're going to get a rag and scrub it all off!*
>
>*Sofia - Are you going to give me an allowance for it?*

Surrendering How I See People

I used to get very distracted by other people, like what they're wearing or doing, how they're behaving - all sorts of things. Likewise, I definitely used to get distracted by things people may have done in the past, sometimes letting anger and judgement take over. I have since realized how that just robs me of any joy and peace I may have, and how I need to learn to see and love others as Jesus does.

I'll use myself attending church in my five-years-ago-mindset, and my more current mindset as examples.

Five years ago:

It's a special evening service hosted by our church, and it's going to start in an hour. I'm helping set up. *"The chairs are not in straight lines. Who did this? This looks horrible! I'll just fix it, like I have to do with so many things, all by myself, I might add.*

Finally, the worship leader is here. Late, as usual, of course. And don't even get me started about the sound guy, who has no clue what he's doing. It sounds so bad that I can't even think straight. There's no sound coming from the main speakers; it's all coming from the crappy monitors. How is anyone supposed to worship with that kind of sound?

Ugh, "Roger" is here early. Why?! He's so irritating. He tries to help, but it just annoys people, mainly me. Just go away, you weirdo. No, I don't want to talk to you. I'm walking away from you."

Service starts. *"Oh great, some of the guests are dancers and flag wavers. I just can't deal with that right now. They drive me crazy; they're so distracting. Why? Why do people think waving flags is a good idea? I can't even concentrate on the worship because all I see are colours flying everywhere. Even when my eyes are closed, I can see some movement through my eyelids. Seriously, stop it. Stop it now.*

Okay, whose kid is crying uncontrollably in the back? Do something with your kid to make it stop. Take him out of

201

the sanctuary; everyone is staring at you. Seriously, why do parents just let their kid scream and don't do anything? Like, be a parent.

Ugh, this guy is speaking? I can't stand him. He was so rude to me a couple of times a while ago, and his comments still make me mad. And then he thinks he's so holy, waltzing in here like he owns the place. Saying he's expecting God to do big things tonight. Yeah, okay. Be nice to me only when you want something, and then expect God to move while you're in charge? I don't think so.

Prayer time. Of course, there's a bunch of people 'laughing in the Spirit', I highly doubt it's real though. Real annoying, more like it. I guess I'll go up for prayer... never mind, I don't want to be prayed for by anyone here.

Well, this service was a waste of time."

Fast forward to now. Since I've been completely broken, I'm trying to allow God to put me back together the only way He can. One of the things I'm learning to surrender is how I see people. I want my thoughts and opinions about people to line up with how God thinks and sees them. I struggle with compassion and empathy, and it's something I've been asking God to help me with for a while now.

A special evening service now; and the mindset I am now striving to maintain:

"I'm here early to see if there's anything I can help with. I'm excited about this service, and it's going to be awesome! Worship practice sounds pretty good. Maybe I'll just stand back here and listen and pray for them while they prepare. God, I ask that you prepare all our hearts to worship in spirit and in truth, no matter what it may sound like. Soften our hearts to be ready to receive what You want to give us tonight.

"Roger" is here. Oh, dear. Lord, please change my heart toward him. Please help me see him the way You see him. That's quite the shirt he has on. Oh, I mean, I surrender any negative thoughts."

Service starts. I close my eyes and sing with my whole heart. My eyes wander over to the flags being waved. I remind myself that it's not about me and my preferences. I close my eyes and start singing again. I purpose my heart and mind to think of the beautiful lyrics I'm singing, and my eyes swell with tears. *"Yes, Father, You truly are overwhelmingly amazing!"*

The speaker starts. *"Lord, You know the things he has said to me in the past. You know how much I wrestle with anger toward him. Please Father, help me to completely surrender my feelings about him to You. It is not for me to judge his motives. I know I can't fully receive what You want to give me here tonight if I still have resentment in my heart. And I know I can't be fully effective for Your kingdom if I haven't completely surrendered every single part of my life. So, I lay this down at Your feet. I give it to You to deal with. Show me how to love him as You love me."*

Prayer time. God is moving everywhere. Some things may not be sincerely real, but it doesn't matter. I'm accountable for only myself. And God has definitely been working on my heart this evening. I want to say that I'm praying for people and people are praying for me, and it's so amazing. But I'm really more of a stand-in-the-back-and-watch, quietly-praying, kind of girl. But even that is amazing. God moves and speaks in all kinds of ways. And tonight, He healed even more of my heart. Afterward, someone quietly comes up to me and shares what God told them about me, and my heart is completely undone. Something I had been praying about was just confirmed through this person, and I am beyond excited.

I leave, completely at peace and overflowing with the joy of the Lord. *"Thank You, Father!"*

SURRENDERING OTHER 'STUFF'

Surrendering My Up-and-Coming 35th Birthday

At the end of June, 2019, I will be 35. I don't feel my age, and as I've mentioned, I still feel like a child in a room full of adults most of the time. In my mind, I still look the same as I did when I was 25. Probably not true, but I can still tell myself that for now. My mom already tells me I'm almost 40. So devastating! Not because 40 is so old, but I feel like I've done nothing with my life, and now it's too late.

I know that's an absolute lie, but sometimes when we feel like we have no hope of going anywhere or doing anything with our life (other than whatever mundane things we're doing now), it can be depressing. Wow, what first-world problems! Still, I love that God cares about the things we care about, no matter how big or little they are.

Conversations with Sofia and Olivia

Ages: 6 and 8

We were driving by the cemetery, and Sofia asked what it was. I explained what it was and what is there.

Olivia - That's so weird that people put their family who've died in the ground.

Me - Well, what else are they going to do with them?

Olivia - I don't know, they could hang them up on their wall or something!

Surrendering My Addiction to Coffee

Just kidding - coffee is life.

SURRENDERING MOVING ON

Surrendering Dating and the New Relationships I've Forced

As I've said before, a couple of months before 2019 began, I knew God's theme word for me for the year would be "new beginnings." Great! *"Maybe I'll meet a cute guy on January 1st, we'll fall in love, and have our new beginning. Sounds perfect."*

Except that didn't happen. I've been alone for what seems to me like an eternity, and I've expressed my frustration to God many, many times. I have three little girls; it sure would be nice to have someone here to help me, back me up, and keep me company. Maybe even mow the grass and fix my fence.

Last year, I could go for a few months of being content by myself. Then I'd have a bit of a meltdown and desperately pray for someone. *"God, I'm tired of raising my girls alone. And I'm tired of being physically alone evening after evening. I'm an extrovert, and I love being around people. I'd love even more to be around someone who wants to be with me as much as I want to be with him. Please send me someone!"*

Then the Lord would lovingly and patiently remind me to surrender it to Him and let Him take care of it. So, I would, for a little while. Then I'd get impatient, *"God You're taking too long, maybe I should help You."* But guess what? God doesn't need our help! Ever. In fact, often, when I tried to help, I just made it worse for myself and put myself in situations I didn't want to be in.

I met a guy at this divorce care class I was attending, and he asked me out for coffee. I initially said yes, but then had this feeling that I shouldn't go. The Lord even gave me an excuse to get out of it, like my babysitter cancelling. Deep down, I knew it was my out, but I ignored it and created a way for a coffee date to happen. Twice. The situation didn't turn out well; lesson learned - the hard way.

When my year of new beginnings came, I thought I'd try online dating. Again, I didn't really have peace about it, and in the back of my heart, I knew I just needed to trust God. But then I wondered if that attitude was just masked fear of stepping out and doing something I've never done before. I met a really nice guy with a good job. He was home from work every night, which was a must for me. (Where I live, most guys work away for long periods of time, as Jake did, and I didn't want that life anymore.) We only went out a couple of times, but again, I had a nudge in my spirit that told me this wasn't right.

I think we doubt those little nudges because we either really want to do things our way, or it just makes sense to us, and every other way doesn't. We try to understand with our human brain how God works, or why He does what He does, or allows to happen what He allows to happen. I'm slowly realizing that trusting Him - even when things don't make sense - is something that He wants us to do. I can try online dating, even though I know it's not something God wants me to do. I can try to be at more places where there are more people (even though that's hard with three small kids and early bedtimes), but ultimately, it's God who will bring me someone who is everything I need and want, and someone who embodies everything important on my list. My list is extensively long and complicated, and in my mind, it's going to be impossible to find that person - especially living where I live. There are a lot of men who live here, but not many Christian men. I've been surrendering my desire for my person, *sometimes every ten minutes*. I have to surrender almost every time I go to the store or anywhere in public because, every time, I wonder if I'm going to meet someone.

There are so many stories in the Bible of how perfect God's plan and timing are. I've been reading the books of the Prophets in the Old Testament lately, so I think of evil King Ahab when he was hit with a random arrow from the opposing army. It was prophesied that he would die in this battle, so he disguised himself as a regular soldier and tried to hide among his fellow men. *But God knew right where he was.* And when the time was right, and Ahab's reign was over, God sent a random arrow flying into a massive field with thousands of other men everywhere, and it hit him. Even more interesting: the opposing army was only interested in killing King Ahab, that's all they had come for. And they had no idea where he was until he was already hit and dying! (1 Kings 22)

When God says He will open doors that no man can open and shut doors that no man can shut, (Isa 22:22) He means it. I've had doubts that I'll find someone who has shared similar experiences with the Lord as I have. I feel like God and I are so close, and I've worked hard at developing such a tight-knit bond with Him. As the Lord calls people deeper and deeper, from glory to glory, it can and often does leave a person with fewer and fewer friends. When God becomes your entire world, you generally have less in common with other people. Likewise, the more conversations you have with God, the less you have to say to people. That's what I've been going through lately, anyways. That said, I believe that God wouldn't put such a strong desire in my heart for Him, and then not provide me with a partner who matches my desires. *"So, Lord, if You could have that done by the end of the day, that'd be great. Thanks. Cough. I mean, sure, all in Your perfect time. Right. Cough. That's what I meant."*

Back to that guy I met online: we messaged a few times after our second date - and were planning a third date - but then he just stopped messaging me. Apparently, this was my first experience being on the *other side* of ghosting. Meh. I've done it to a couple of people before, so I guess it was my turn. When we first met, I toyed with the idea of mellowing down my faith because he wasn't into it as much. Looking back, I'm really disappointed with myself for even considering that, especially after all Christ has done and been for me these last couple of years. Having to surrender that shame was harder. Needless to say, I cancelled my online dating account and will not be making another one.

I'm trying to rest in the confidence that God will do what He's promised me - when the time is right. The dreams and scriptures He's given to me will come to pass. *Any decade now...*

Conversations with Sofia

Age: 5.5

> *I overhear Olivia and Sofia arguing, and as the bickering got louder and louder, I hear:*
>
> *Olivia - Sofia, you can't do that!*
>
> *Sofia - YOU DON'T KNOW ME! YOU DON'T KNOW MY LIFE!*

Surrendering My List

When I was in my very early twenties, I felt the Lord tell me to make a list of what I was looking for in a husband. I did but felt a little weird doing it because I felt like I didn't deserve what I was looking for or what I wanted. When I met Jake, I looked back on my list and noticed he didn't match a few things on it. Oh well, I thought, maybe it doesn't really matter. Maybe I was asking too much.

You know how annoying it is to go to the grocery store and forget to get some of the important things on your list? You don't realize it until you get home, have unloaded all the kids and groceries, can't find the milk and eggs, and then realize you forgot to get them. So, you pack up the kids - again - and head out to the store - again. By this time, you're frustrated and tired, the baby is hungry, tired, and crying, and the other kids are arguing in the back seat about who mommy loves more, and now they're both crying. Back into the store you go. By the time you've picked up these once-forgotten items, and you're paying for them, all your children are having fits and you're debating giving them all to the next person in line! Things sure would have been so easier if you would have just remembered to get everything on your list the *first time*.

The "What-I-want-in-a-husband" list: in the last couple of years, I've worked on making a new one; it's very detailed and specific, and somewhat unrealistic. I know what I want and the desires the Lord has placed in my heart, and I've come to realize that I will not be able to find that kind of man on my own. God will have to bring him to me. My list is similar to the one that I had in my twenties, but also very different, since having children changes priorities in terms of what I'm looking for - as do past life events. Some things are more important now, and some things aren't, but the biggest difference is now, *I won't deviate from my list.* I will not settle, no matter how long it takes. If you find yourself falling for someone who isn't passionately in love with the Lord like you are, and it's important to you that they are - as it should be - do not settle, no matter what! If you find yourself falling for someone who says they love God, but doesn't treat you well, turn around and run far away!

Last year, I almost settled for an old friend from back in third grade. We went to the same schools through graduation, in choir together in high school, and there was always some chemistry between us. Fast forward to January 2018, and here he is again. He fulfilled about 80 percent of the requirements on my list. I didn't think I'd find someone better, but I always had this check in my spirit. After hanging out together a few months (never officially dating because neither one of us was legally divorced), I just knew it wasn't right, but I couldn't pull myself away. The 20 percent lacking didn't seem like a huge amount, but it was still important to me, still a big deal. Although it took me a while to figure it out, and a few times of God specifically telling me no, we eventually parted ways. God was serious enough about it because He caused him to move eight hours away, which I knew was for the better. We're still good friends and often talk - even joke about wishing we were right for each other - but we both know we're not what God has planned for either one of us.

I've come to learn that God cares so much about the details of our lives. He cares about my must-have list for the impossible guy to find, so I wrote it out, gave it to Him, and then completely surrendered it to Him. While it may look impossible to me, that's where God works the best, and I want people who know my story to see and know that only God could have orchestrated how He brought my future husband and me together, in His timing. I want people to see what the Father's heart looks like when they see us together and how much we love each other. I want people to see how a loving God can take our brokenness, mending, and forming something so beautiful. I want people to see how redemptive God truly is, and I want the Father to be glorified in *every area of our relationship.*

If you're in a similar situation, I encourage you to ask God to help you make a list of what you are looking for in your forever person. You can add things you'd *like to have*, but don't let them be deal-breakers. Be specific about the traits and matters that are important to you, but also seek the Lord about what He wants for you. Once you've completed your list, hand it over to the Lord, completely surrendering it to Him, trusting Him that He will bring you the right person at the right time. Any time you have a check in your spirit, *listen to it.* Any time you feel like you may have the green light to do something (like online dating), step out and do it. Stay in constant communion with God; as your relationship with Him gets stronger, He'll give you the desires of your heart.

This is my very detailed list that I will NOT deviate from:

My Absolute Must-Haves:

- Be completely in love with Jesus
- Be completely in love with me and treat me amazingly
- Must be home from work every night - wake up with me in the morning and go to bed with me at night
- Love my girls like they're his own and treat them well
- Very involved as a step-dad - being a godly example and showing them how they should be treated by other men

- Both of us proud to be with each other - like when going out in public
- Honest and loyal - I must be able to trust him completely
- Loves my body and thinks I'm beautiful no matter what shape I'm in
- Helps around the house
- We must have amazing conversation and open communication
- My family has to love him, and he has to love spending time with them because we're very close
- Theologically similar - as well as a similar *style* of worship
- Wants to do things with me, even if it's just going to the grocery store, for a walk, or taking the girls to the park

Surrendering Love Again

In the process of writing and editing this book, I met someone wonderful. He's everything I've ever wanted, everything on my list, and more. Kris is my perfect puzzle piece, fitting me perfectly. Guess where we met? At my church - the least likely place that I thought I'd meet someone! A few months before we met, during prayer, I told God that if He didn't want me to go to another church to meet someone, He would have to bring my man to me. And He did! Our church hosted a city-wide worship night on March 1, 2019, and I felt like I not only needed to go but also help my sister lead worship. I didn't want to, but wanting to be obedient more, I went.

I walked through the doors, and he was already there, sitting in the back. He looked back at me, doing a very noticeable double-take with a sort of panicked look in his eyes. Later, I found out why: eight months before, he had seen me in the mall and couldn't stop thinking about me since - and now, there I was! I noticed him that night at church, and feelings for him started popping up.

"Hmm, this is weird. What is happening to me? Why can't I stop thinking about him? I don't even know him!"

I introduced myself to him and walked away, but we kept exchanging glances the entire night. Nothing came of it that night, so I prayed. *"Lord, I don't know what's happening in my heart, but I surrender it all to you. If something is supposed to come of this, he knows where I go to church, so he'll have to come on Sunday."* Well, he didn't come that Sunday, or for another three Sundays after that, so I just left it alone. Little did I know that God was working in Kris' heart the entire time, asking him to wait before returning to my church when the time was right. When he did start coming to my church, the timing was perfect, with things falling into place completely - and quickly (God completely redeemed what I thought was lost time). We started dating not long afterward.

Kris, not unlike every other person in the world, has a past. When we made our relationship public on social media, I was immediately messaged about his past, as if I didn't know. A frustrating aspect of Christianity is that we believe that God can and does heal and redeem people and their past - we pray for it all the time - but sometimes, when it does happen, we don't fully believe it, or we can't stop reminding others about their past. And they thought they were finally free from it! In our case though, Kris and I are both free from our pasts, God has redeemed us both, and no matter what anyone says, God has called us to move forward.

The day after I received a message about Kris, I prayed, asking God for confirmation whether what we were doing was - in fact - what He wanted. I didn't want to waste anyone's time, getting our hopes up, just to be disappointed. That same night, Kris came over after prayer meeting, and while we were talking, he mentioned that he was so proud to be with me that he couldn't wait to take me out in public and show me off to the world. While I was flattered, my mind immediately went back to when Jake didn't want to hold my hand in public because "it looked stupid." Or when the guy I *almost* dated last year had to pick up something from his sister's place and chose to park beside some trees so his sister wouldn't see that I was with him. As I conveyed these

224

stories to Kris, he closed his eyes and smiled a sort of painful smile. I thought he was going to tell me to get over it, just like I had been told so many times before, but instead, he said, "When I was on my flight to Arizona last week, I was praying, and the Lord told me that He wanted me to apologize on behalf all of the men who didn't know how to cherish you. When they broke your heart, they broke God's heart too. He also told me that He wanted me to wash your feet and pray for you and with you. He said He wants to download something into your heart through this act of vulnerability and service in humility. This will be significant for both you and the girls and be like a covering over them. I saw a picture of you sitting in your chair in your living room, and me washing your feet. I've been waiting for the right time, and I believe it's now. I've never done anything like this before, and feel a bit awkward about it, but would you mind if I washed your feet?"

I sat there staring at him, totally dumbfounded, yet completely moved. *"Yes! I would absolutely love that!"*

Just in case you've never heard about it before, I'd like to explain the meaning behind feet-washing. I knew it was special but didn't know all the details about it until doing some research, myself. Feet washing is probably one of the most significant, yet humble, things a person can do for someone else. It is a pure display of servanthood. In John 13, Jesus, knowing that the Father had given Him all control and power over all things, got up from the table and humbly washed the disciples' feet, demonstrating pure, unconditional love and servanthood *to His own servants*. He then called them (as well as present-day *us*) to do likewise, serving one another in love and humility.

In ancient Jewish times, sandals were often used in covenants of inheritance. The footnote in TPT for John 13:7 says, "Every defilement would be removed so that they could 'place the sole of their feet' upon the new covenant inheritance."[10] So, Jesus' act of taking off their sandals and washing their feet signifies removing the old

---

[10] Simmons, Dr. Brian. The Passion Translation. BroadStreet Publishing, LLC. 2017. Pg. 626

inheritance, washing them clean, and then giving them a new life-giving inheritance - which was Himself.

When Kris knelt at my feet, putting them in the water, I was a little self-conscious at first because I had stubble above my ankles around my ridiculously flat feet. (But I had pretty bright pink nail polish, so I want to say it cancels that out!) Either way, none of that mattered. As Kris rubbed my feet in the water and prayed for me, I felt something in my spirit completely release, and tears began to come. I wept and wept as the shame began to leave, replaced with unconditional, pure love. I was completely overwhelmed by God's kindness, gifting me with the most beautiful, meaningful moment I have ever experienced in my life. I finally knew what it meant to be completely, unconditionally loved by a man.

As he dried my feet, we both cried and prayed. I knew this was the confirmation I was looking for. Everything I had gone through in my life was leading up to this beautiful moment of redemption. And as time has passed, I've realized even more so the significance of that event. I've been given a new inheritance. And not only

227

me, but my girls as well. All our heartache and brokenness were washed away, and a new life was given. Our mourning has been turned into dancing.

It's important that we make a list of what we need and want in our spouse, and once we realize our own worth, it's harder to stray from the list because we know we don't deserve anything *less than God's best*. Things that are important to us are important to Him; He cares about the details. I wanted someone who was madly in love with God and me and would love and cherish my girls as if they were his own. I almost settled a few times in the last three years, but every time God reminded me what it was like when I settled the first time, and what stemmed from that. Though I'd never change my past (I have three of the most amazing girls in the world), I know I'll never settle again. Kris is everything on my list and even more things that I didn't even realize I wanted.

It's the year of new beginnings, and I am beyond excited for what God has up his sleeve for my family. I've fully surrendered everything about my relationship with Kris to God. Everything has been dependent on His timing and has worked out so effortlessly so far. We've been moving forward quickly - which we both knew would happen. We are right where God wants us to be, completely surrendered to His will, unbelievably happy, and at peace.

I had an idea that when I did find my person, I wouldn't struggle with feeling down or wouldn't need to pray as much because I'd have someone to talk to now. That was a juvenile way of thinking, as if I wouldn't be fully happy until I found the right person. The truth is that that it's more important than ever to pray now. When God brings two people together, giving them a purpose, the enemy will try and distract them or break them apart. Kris and I have learned to guard our relationship (now, marriage) against the enemy, always putting Christ first, because without Christ at front and center, our relationship becomes strained. It is awesome how much we love each other and how close we are when He is first in our lives.

Yes, you read that right: we got married! We met and were married six months later - to the day. While some thought we were crazy, we knew it was right. We had both been single for a while, we both knew what we wanted - and what we *didn't want* - in a relationship. More importantly, we both felt very strongly that we were led by the Holy Spirit.

Both individually and together, we've learned to surrender everything to the Lord. Everything from our family's responses to our dating and very quick engagement / marriage, to raising our kids together in a blended family. Kris is learning how to deal with my girls' rainbows of emotions, and I am learning how to love and show patience to his two teenage kids. We've surrendered so many things and will continue surrendering until we're old and grey. I still must surrender everything I've written in this book, almost every day!

I'm very, very happy. It was a long process, and while I had learned to be content single, I'm thrilled to now be married to such a wonderful, kind, and thoughtful man. If he gets called in to work on a Saturday morning, he'll stop and get me a coffee on the way home. He always looks for ways to spend time with me, even if it's just going to the grocery store to get a couple of things, he'll come in with me and push the cart. We lay in bed at night, talking until he falls asleep. I like to make Kris laugh so hard his whole face turns purple. We love to talk about different things the Lord has been showing us or teaching us. Sometimes we go to our church and crank up some worship music and just worship together. We both enjoy and look forward to family dinners or get-togethers. He really is my perfect puzzle piece. I am so, so grateful that the Lord redeemed us both and gave us each another chance. God is a good, good Father.

Conversations with Sofia

Age: 5

One morning before swimming lessons, I was brushing Sofia's hair and putting it in a French braid.

Sofia - Ow, mom! Why do you have to brush my hair?! You don't even know what's going on in my life right now!

Me - Ok, what's going on in your life?

Sofia - You're brushing my hair, and it hurts! It's the worst thing that's ever happened in my whole life!

Surrendering the "Now What?"

This chapter is an after-thought. Often, when I can't sleep at night (which is frequently), God gives me different ideas or inspirations. Most of the time I can't fall back sleep until I write them down. But I knew I wouldn't forget this one because it's a topic that I think about pretty much every minute of the day: now what?

Again, the Lord has asked me to wait and trust Him with every aspect of my life. After a year and a half of writing and editing, my manuscript is finally finished and edited as much as I can do. I've spoken with a couple of different publishers and have been given quotes as to how much it will cost to get it into the hands of readers. I don't have the money to do it - not even remotely. I'm more than willing to get a job, saving up to pay the bills we already have and also to pay for getting this book published. Still, God has asked me to surrender, wait, and trust. So for now, a year and a half of work, sits nicely on my desk, in a teal coloured three ring binder.

I've recently gone back and read the manuscript quite a while after writing it, and was both challenged and encouraged in my faith. I've realized that surrendering many aspects of my life are going to be life-long lessons I'll be forever learning. And that's okay. I'm just grateful God loves me enough to never give up on me.

I have a delicious recipe for cupcakes and frosting, and many have encouraged me to start a baking business, so I've been giving that a lot of thought lately. It would be fun and also give me something to do, maybe even give me a sense of purpose and keep me from wandering around like a lost puppy, wondering what I'm doing with my life! Again, the Lord has asked me to surrender, wait, and trust.

I love being married. It's really hard, and some days are better than others. Blending our two very different families has proven to be quite the undertaking! But Kris is my absolute best friend and biggest supporter in everything. I still sometimes feel guilty that I'm not working. Kris works hard, and I feel like I should, too, especially now that we have more bills. He's never made me feel guilty for not working - that's all me. In my way of thinking, there's no reason why I can't work! But time and time again, God has asked me to surrender, wait, and trust.

So here I sit. Surrendering. Waiting. Trusting. At least, I'm trying to, but it's one of the hardest things to do! Especially right now when money has become really scarce; bills aren't going away, and there's no room left on the credit cards. I know God is trying to teach me to trust His timing, so if I could just learn it now and move on with life, that'd be great.

Deep breath. Exhale. Surrender everything. Wait. Trust Him. Rest in complete peace, knowing God lavishly loves us and is taking care of absolutely everything.

Made in the USA
Middletown, DE
22 March 2021